EFFECTIVE THINKING® FOR UNCOMMON SUCCESS

The ET Process for Uncommon Success

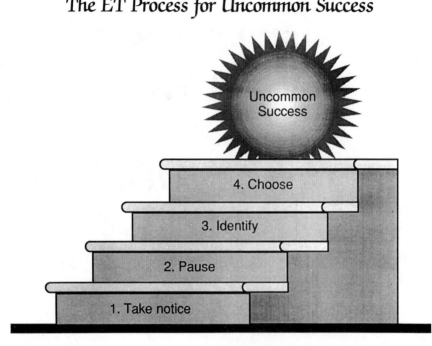

EFFECTIVE THINKING® FOR UNCOMMON SUCCESS

Gerald Kushel

American Management Association

This publication is designed to provide accurate and authoritative information in regard to the subject matter covered. It is sold with the understanding that the publisher is not engaged in rendering legal, accounting, or other professional service. If legal advice or other expert assistance is required, the services of a competent professional person should be sought.

Library of Congress Cataloging-in-Publication Data

Kushel, Gerald.
  Effective thinking for uncommon success / Gerald Kushel.
    p. cm.
Includes index.
ISBN 0-8144-5964-1
1. Success. 2. Thought and thinking. I. Title
BF637.S8K87 1991   90-55205
158'.1—dc20   CIP

EFFECTIVE THINKING and EFFECTIVE THINKING PROCESS are registered trademarks of Gerald Kushel.

Contents

Acknowledgments

Thanks first of all to my dear wife, Selma, who helped me develop and refine the ideas in this book from the earliest stages. Selma is not only my wife of thirty-three years and my best friend, she is also a colleague. Together we have had a great deal of excitement, challenge, and pleasure in conducting many workshops and seminars on the ET process over recent years.

I would also like to thank my editor at AMACOM, Andrea Pedolsky, who served as a sounding board, helping me clarify many of the key concepts in this book. Her generous help and constructive critique throughout the writing period are deeply appreciated. Also, I wish to thank departmental colleagues and close friends who generously shared ideas; particularly Dr. Roy Smith, Dr. Stan Friedland, Dr. Daniel Araoz, Stan Brodsky, and Dr. Arnold Raisner. Of course I alone am responsible for any shortcomings in this work.

My deepest thanks goes, to all the uncommonly successful people who confided in me and shared their uncommon way of thinking to solve problems and issues. Without them this book would never have been possible.

EFFECTIVE THINKING® FOR UNCOMMON SUCCESS

Chapter 1

Effective Thinking:
Your Foundation for a
Successful Life

[Describes the study of uncommonly successful people—the relatively few who have achieved success in three dimensions: high job performance, high level of job satisfaction, and high level of satisfaction with personal life. Highlights three key ingredients of uncommon success: inner calm, clarity of purpose, and sense of adventure. Introduces the four-step effective thinking process, and explains certain key aspects. Provides self-test to measure present level of effective thinking and pinpoint areas for improvement. Explains three important assumptions necessary to begin learning the effective thinking process.]

The title of this book was chosen with care: *Effective Thinking for Uncommon Success*. "Uncommon success" means simultaneous success in three significant dimensions:

1. Successful performance on the job
2. High level of personal satisfaction at work
3. Success in personal and family life

It is not unusual to encounter people who are outstanding performers on the job, or who find a great sense of satisfaction in their work, or have rich and fulfilling personal lives. What is uncommon is finding someone who is successful in *all three* dimensions. Uncommonly successful people (I call them USPs) are, by definition, rare.

How do they manage it? They have an unusual way of thinking. Either intuitively or by having learned it, all USPs practice what I call "effective thinking." And you can learn it too. Effective thinking is not the same as positive thinking. An effective thought is one that helps you accomplish what you want; it is *effective* at bringing you success—however you measure it—in all three dimensions of your life.

The underlying premise of this book is that what you think about the situations that you encounter in life determines how you feel, and how you feel, in turn, determines how you behave. Whenever you are involved in a certain situation—at work, at home, wherever—certain thoughts about that situation go through your mind. Those thoughts can range from very positive to quite negative, but in every case they set the stage for what you *do* in that situation. And your overall feeling that your life is or is not going well comes from the cumulative total of all those events. It's not too simplified to say it this way: You are very much in charge of the way you think and it is the *way* you think that has everything to do with your level of success!

Right about here a lot of people look at me as if they think I'm not all there but are too polite to say so. "But I can't help the way I think," they're saying to themselves; "I can't control my thoughts. Who does this guy think he is?"

Well, you *can* control what you think. Whatever thoughts you have in your mind belong entirely to you, and to no one else. So who controls your thoughts, if not you? We will be going into this idea of *choosing* your thoughts in some detail later, but for now let me answer the other question: Who does this guy think he is?

For the past twenty-three years, I have been a university professor, conducting graduate courses in mental health counseling and career development. During that time, I have also maintained a private practice in psychotherapy. In addition, since 1979, as a management consultant I have conducted hundreds of business seminars on personal and corporate effectiveness throughout the United States and Europe.

What I know about the connection between thoughts and feelings, between intellect and emotion, comes from my years as a mental health educator and practitioner. My ideas about effective thinking, and in particular the four-step process that is explained in this book, have evolved over a decade of working with high-performing individuals and groups.

A Profile of the Uncommonly Successful Person

Over the years I have conducted an ongoing experiment with graduate students, clients, and people who have participated in my business seminars. I selected people who were obviously high performers in their profession or trade, and asked them to participate in an informal study of three-dimensional success. They already had one dimension filled, and I wanted to understand what the rest of their life was like.

In total, 1,200 people have been studied, all of them very successful at their jobs. Most were high-level business executives, but there were also physicians, school administrators and educators, lawyers, artists, and a number of high performing white- and blue-collar workers from various settings. Sixty percent were male, ranging in age from twenty-one to seventy-six. They were all administered a job satisfaction inventory *and* a personal life satisfaction inventory, and the results were quite fascinating.

Sixteen percent (192) had low scores on *both* inventories. It seemed to me that they were on a path to early burnout, or perhaps an early grave.

Eighty percent (960) scored in the middle range or lower

on one or both of the inventories—what I would consider only semisuccessful. Many in this group scored quite high in job satisfaction but very low in personal life satisfaction. This is not really surprising; we all know many people who sacrifice their personal life in order to succeed professionally. (One interviewee answered my inquiry about his personal life satisfaction by saying, "Personal life? What is that? I have no personal life.") But also included in this semisuccessful group were people who scored low on job satisfaction but high in the quality of their personal life. It seems that most of us tend to fit into this semisuccessful category. Isn't it common to believe that you can't have it all, that there has to be compromise?

However, there was one group, a very small group, who scored high in all three areas. Forty-eight people (4 percent) out of the entire sample of 1,200 were clearly enjoying uncommon, three-dimensional success. They were all very good at what they do for a living, *and* they really enjoyed that work, *and* on top of that they had very rich and satisfying personal lives. Of course I realize this is not a scientific study and that it is not based on a truly random sample. But I believe it fair to generalize that uncommonly successful people represent a very small segment of our general population.

Once I identified the members of this 4 percent group of USPs, I tried to learn as much as possible about them. I interviewed them all and, when possible, observed them on the job and in certain aspects of their personal life. Many participated in small-group, intensive, week-long seminars that I conducted, so I got to know them quite well. I wanted to know what made it possible for them to be so internally successful in all dimensions, when so many others were not doing nearly as well. Was there a special factor, or unique combination of factors, that enabled them to do so extraordinarily well, both professionally and personally? Or were they just lucky?

Indeed I found one major factor common to all—and it

wasn't luck. Every one of the USPs that I studied has *a relatively uncommon way of thinking*. All were, in their own way, masters of the effective thinking process—the process that I will share with you in this book. Most of them were not "natural born" effective thinkers. A few were, but most of them had developed their effective thinking after overcoming various setbacks of one kind or another.

But doing it the "hard way" is not essential. I have found that the effective thinking process can readily be passed on to others. If you decide to do so, you can, in relatively short order, learn how to use the process to achieve your own very high level of uncommon, three-dimensional success.

The Three Keys to Satisfaction

In addition to effective thinking (or we might say *because* of it), all the USPs in my study had three other qualities in common:

1. Inner calm
2. Clarity of purpose
3. A sense of adventure

All the USPs whom I studied shared these life-enriching qualities. All had a great deal of inner peace. They had a clear sense of mission and purpose in their lives. And their lives were clearly providing them with plenty of fun and adventure.

Interestingly, all three of these qualities can be achieved by the kind of thinking that you do. USPs testify that the *calmer* they become, the easier it is for them to understand their life's purpose. And the clearer their purposes become, the easier it is for them to become spontaneous, to take risks, and to have fun and adventure in their life.

Attaining a balance of these three qualities is a clear goal of most USPs, and it makes a great deal of sense for you to set that as a goal for yourself.

Can you expect to thrive without having inner peace? Not likely. And if you do not have a sense of purpose you will most certainly feel very empty. And even if you have inner calm and purpose, can you be really happy without adventure in your life? You need a balance of all three if you are to attain a maximum level of life satisfaction.

Three-Dimensional Success That Lasts a Lifetime

All uncommonly successful people want the same thing, at rock bottom: They want to have the very best life possible. This is where everything starts. This underlying goal means different things to different people, of course, but to USPs it always means achieving success in the three key dimensions. And they expect to achieve *lasting* success.

Is there really such a thing as lasting success? Very definitely—if you are referring to success in personal and professional quality of life—that is the goal of USPs. Their success is durable because they and they alone control it.

Success Dimension 1—High Job Performance

For USPs, "high job performance" is based entirely on criteria that are under their full control. All the USPs in my study were rated "high performers" by their bosses, but at bottom, it was more important that they feel proud of their *own* accomplishments. That is why success in terms of job performance is long lasting for USPs; they always work up to the high standards that they set for themselves. Even after they retire, USPs are high performers—at least on their own terms.

Success Dimension 2—A High Level of Job Satisfaction

Job satisfaction level is entirely a matter of attitude, not external factors. And people who practice effective thinking can control their attitude. Therefore USPs through effective thinking, guarantee themselves enjoyment of their work, no matter how difficult it might look to the outsider.

Success Dimension 3—A High Level of Satisfaction in Personal Life

Satisfaction with one's personal life is largely a matter of attitude—which is a matter of effective thinking. USPs make it their business to have an excellent attitude about their personal life, regardless of how difficult things might get.

So we see that job satisfaction and personal life satisfaction are strictly internal dimensions, and high job performance is based on standards set by USPs themselves. Thus all three dimensions of the success of USPs are entirely under their control. And so they can, if they want to, realistically assure themselves that three-dimensional success will last them for a lifetime.

Overview of the Effective Thinking Process

The effective thinking process has four very distinct steps:

Step 1:   TAKE NOTICE. You note that you are not moving in the way that you intended toward your goal of uncommon success. Something is interfering with success in one, or perhaps more, of the three key dimensions.

Step 2:   PAUSE. Mentally take time out. Stop whatever you've been thinking and force yourself to reconsider. In other words, you must stop to examine and break your goal-defeating mindset. Depending on the work that needs to be done in step 3, the pause can be anywhere from a few seconds to a number of months. During the pause you focus on just one issue, while the rest of your life goes on as always.

Step 3:   IDENTIFY. Find—or create—the effective thought necessary to replace the defective thoughts that are defeating your progress toward uncommon success. An effective thought is any thought that leads you directly or indirectly toward the goal of uncommon success. To be effective, a thought does not have to be "brilliant" or "correct;" all it has to do is lead you toward the goal. A defective thought is the opposite: any thought that *fails* to lead you directly or indirectly toward the uncommon success goal that you have set for yourself.

Step 4:   CHOOSE. From the effective thoughts that you identified in step 3, you actively choose effective thoughts to replace your defective thoughts.

The ET Process is shown graphically in Figure 1–1.

Let's consider an example. Suppose you find that John, a colleague, is periodically leaning over your shoulder to peer at the work you are doing. This tends to spoil your concentration. Not only that, you find his behavior very annoying. In fact, you fear that he might be "borrowing" some of your best ideas. We'll assume that you've asked John several times to stop looking at your work, but the annoying behavior continues.

Time to engage in the ET process. Move to step 1 (take notice) by quietly asking yourself, "Considering the fact that

Figure 1-1. The four-step effective thinking process.®

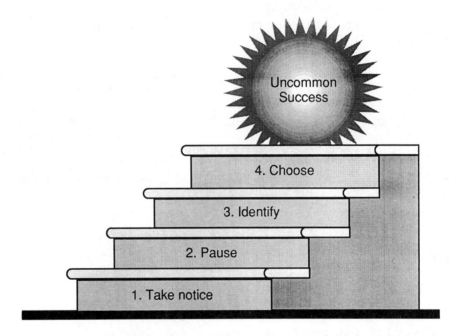

John's behavior seems to be getting the best of me, can I honestly say that I am currently living the life of an uncommonly successful person?" If you conclude that in spite of John's behavior you are still very much on the path to uncommon success, you need to go no further with the process. But if you feel that you are off track, then go immediately to step 2—pause.

One way to pause is simply to say to yourself, "Stop. Stop making yourself so upset." That statement alone will help you break your goal-defeating mindset. Once you have reminded yourself that it is you who are making yourself upset and not John, you will be back on the track toward your goal. It is during step 2 that you initiate step 3—identify.

Step 3 involves some serious problem solving. Your job is to identify the defective thoughts about John that are upsetting you, and replace them with effective thoughts that do not upset you, thoughts that will put you back on track. All of your emotional upset, as you shall see, is caused by your thoughts and your thoughts alone. For example, you might have been thinking:

> "John's personality is most definitely getting on my nerves."
> "I can't stand anyone looking over my shoulder when I am doing detailed work."
> "I'm afraid that John will steal my ideas and present them to the boss as his own and then I won't get the appreciation I deserve."

First, you might want to consider some effective thoughts that will lead to appropriate action:

> "If John persists in this behavior, I'll straighten him out in no uncertain terms. I'll try using very firm language that will get through to him, and if that doesn't work, I'll report him to the boss."
> "I'll ask to have his work station changed."
> "I'll arrange to have my work station changed."

At the same time, make a mental list of some other effective thoughts:

> "I'll simply ignore him."
> "It is not John's personality that is upsetting me, but rather my thoughts about John's personality that are upsetting me. Therefore, let me remind myself to see aspects of John's personality that are not particularly upsetting."
> "John is trying hard to make the most of his limited ability and needs all the help he can get."
> "I am a fountain of new ideas. If John wants to steal my

ideas, that's okay; there are plenty more where these came from."

"John is a known quantity in this office and so am I. The boss knows the quality of my work. I have nothing to worry about."

Once you have completed the necessary detective work of identifying defective thoughts and effective thoughts, you move to the fourth and final step: Actively choose an effective thought or thoughts from among those that you have identified. "Choosing" requires active will power. That may seem far-fetched right now, but I assure you it is possible. In the pages ahead, I will show you a number of proven ways for actively choosing effective thoughts.

All four steps of the ET process can be compressed into just two sentences: *Take notice of when you are not moving toward uncommon success, and then pause. Then identify and* choose *effective thoughts.*

Understanding the ET Process

The fundamental concepts underlying the theory of effective thinking may well be new to you, and you probably have a few questions. This first chapter, which is intended to be an orientation, is an appropriate place to describe some of the key points about the ET process.

• *You are responsible for your thoughts*. The central ingredient in effective thinking is willingness to take total self-responsibility—not for everything that goes on in the world, but simply 100 percent responsibility for your own thoughts, your own feelings, and your own behavior. In essence, USPs say, "Neither she, he, it, nor they ever make me feel or act in a particular way. It is the thoughts that I choose that do the trick, that make me feel terrific or make me get sick.''

• *Effective thinking is more than positive thinking.* Don't confuse effective thinking with Pollyanna-style positive thinking. Effective thinking often incorporates the best elements of realistic positive thinking, but it also has the best elements of creative negative thinking. Positive thinking, of course, can be very helpful. But when it is naïve, saccharine, or overly idealistic, it can be quite harmful, even dangerous.

USPs prefer to realistically face the hardships of life directly and then take appropriate action to change things for the better. If you feel a suspicious growth in your abdomen, the wise course is to see a physician, not simply to "think positively." If you have negative data that suggest it is time to move out of the stock market, that's the time to take action—not to wait passively and "think positively."

• *The ET process is results-oriented.* Effective thinking is a very down-to-earth, practical, results-oriented kind of thinking. The word *effective* literally means getting results. It doesn't really matter if the thoughts you choose are brilliant or not very clear, logical or illogical, or even "right" or "wrong," as long as they work. With effective thinking, all that really matters is, did the thought you chose do the job you wanted it to? Did it produce the result you were after? If the thinking that you do moves you toward your goal of personal and professional success, and *not at the expense of anyone else,* then it is, by definition, effective.

• *Even negative thinking can sometimes be highly effective.* USP George Barth was asked to prepare a very important report for his company.* Instead of permitting himself to feel overconfident, he *deliberately* made himself worry,

*Most of the examples, and cases used in this book are taken directly from interviews with USPs and from my clients. They openly and candidly shared their private ideas and perspectives with me, and I am honor-bound to protect their privacy by using fictitious names and changing small details to disguise their identities.

and that "creative worry" gave him the extra incentive for an all-out effort. Result: a superior report.

Even anger-producing and depressing thoughts can be effective. For example, to get over the loss of anything that is important to you, you must permit yourself to get depressed, if only for a short time. USPs, therefore, quite deliberately choose thoughts to make themselves depressed or angry when they experience losses in life so that they can expedite their acceptance of that loss, and be ready to move on.

▪ *Effective thinking builds on conventional thinking.* While effective thinking incorporates the best from all kinds of thinking, including certain kinds of positive thinking, it emphasizes facing up to the harsh realities of your personal and professional life—and then moving forward, as best you can, from whatever position you happen to be in. Effective thinking builds on the conventional thinking that most people do but then shifts that thinking ever so slightly whenever appropriate. With just a slight twist or unusual emphasis, you can make your everyday thinking much more fruitful.

For example, when a USP faces a setback, he thinks to himself, That wasn't a failure, it was a learning opportunity. An effective thinker will capitalize on his occasional negative thinking, but will redefine it as creative worry, "selective guilt, or healthy anger" whenever it makes sense to do so. USPs use creative worry to get their adrenalin pumping so they can meet the deadline or attend to family responsibilities.

▪ *Effective thinking provides for our individual differences.* The thought that proves effective for one person may not work at all for another. Whether a thought is effective for you depends on two factors: (1) your own unique and special tastes and (2) the particular results that you are after. Remember, a given thought, whether it is deliberately chosen or automatically emerges, will be classified as "defective" (no matter how brilliant) if it does not produce the outcome that thinker hoped to achieve.

In some instances, then, the thinking that is effective for me may not be at all effective for you, and vice versa. What is effective for you depends very much on your own style, preferences, and personal history. That's one of the things about effective thinking that I believe you will appreciate the most. You'll have your own brand.

▪ *There is an effective thought for any situation that life dishes up.* Effective thinking will help change your perception of a given situation in a way that will have maximum payoff for you. That doesn't mean that you'll just accept anything that happens to you. It means that you will readily accept those things that you can do nothing about and preserve your energy for the things that you *can* do something about—and there are many. You'll be surprised at how easy it will become, with just a little practice, to identify an effective thought, or series of effective thoughts, for any difficult situation that you face at home or at work.

You probably have been using the ET process quite naturally in some parts of your life already. If you've accomplished anything worthwhile in your life, you have undoubtedly already done a great deal of effective thinking—even though you probably didn't call it that and might not even have been aware of the process. If you wanted to complete college and did it, much of your success goes to the effective thinking that you did intuitively. If you set out to land your present job and you did, that too was a product of your own effective thinking. What we'll be doing in this book is simply systematizing this kind of thinking, showing you how you can employ it consistently for uncommon success.

The ET Self-Test

Our goal with this book is to show you how to think effectively so that you can achieve uncommon, three-dimensional success. But, as I mentioned, many people do some amount of effective thinking quite naturally, and no doubt you are one. So our first step is to rate your present level of effective thinking with this self-test. It will help you identify areas in your present ways of thinking that might benefit from change. You can then concentrate on those areas as you learn more about the ET process.

To take the test, simply circle the number that most closely approximates your current agreement or disagreement with the statement above it. Be as honest with yourself as possible.

The USP Self-Test

1. I tend to believe that I have projects but no lasting problems. I quickly turn any problem into a project.

   9   8   7   6   5   4   3   2   1
   Agree   *Disagree*

2. I tend to think of myself as perhaps a bit skeptical but never cynical.

   9   8   7   6   5   4   3   2   1
   Agree   *Disagree*

3. I have a clear inner identity that is not predicated on my job or my title, or even my family role.

   9   8   7   6   5   4   3   2   1
   Agree   *Disagree*

4. I think of myself as being a very realistic person, as opposed to a very reasonable person.

   9   8   7   6   5   4   3   2   1
   Agree   *Disagree*

5. I tend to believe that I have relatively few real "failures," but instead, I have "learning opportunities."

   9   8   7   6   5   4   3   2   1
   Agree   *Disagree*

6. I often seek to influence others, but I never seriously expect to or need to "control" others.

    9   8   7   6   5   4   3   2   1
    Agree   *Disagree*

7. I am often caring and concerned, but rarely guilt-ridden or worried.

    9   8   7   6   5   4   3   2   1
    Agree   *Disagree*

8. I feel empathy rather than mere sympathy for people who are experiencing some difficulty.

    9   8   7   6   5   4   3   2   1
    Agree   *Disagree*

9. I am more concerned about making wise decisions than merely making quick decisions. Yet I am quite decisive.

    9   8   7   6   5   4   3   2   1
    Agree   *Disagree*

10. I have many preferences, but relatively few real needs.

    9   8   7   6   5   4   3   2   1
    Agree   *Disagree*

11. I do not see people as genuinely lazy, only as insufficiently moviated.

    9   8   7   6   5   4   3   2   1
    Agree   *Disagree*

12. I may have due concern about impending difficulties, but I seldom have excessive worry.

9   8   7   6   5   4   3   2   1
Agree   Disagree

13. I use my own anger constructively. I realize that, at bottom, all anger stems from fear. Since I realize that I generally have very little to fear, I rarely get angry.

9   8   7   6   5   4   3   2   1
Agree   Disagree

14. I take a two-pronged attack on job-related difficulties: effective action plus an effective attitude.

9   8   7   6   5   4   3   2   1
Agree   Disagree

15. I consider myself a "thought chooser" rather than a victim of any thought that happens to come to mind. I use every means I know of to help me take charge of my thinking.

9   8   7   6   5   4   3   2   1
Agree   Disagree

16. No matter what my present state of mind, I still reserve the right to believe that the best is yet to come.

9   8   7   6   5   4   3   2   1
Agree   Disagree

17. I am a risk taker, but I take the kinds of risks that add to, rather than detract from, the quality of my inner life.

9   8   7   6   5   4   3   2   1
Agree   Disagree

18. I see my life as a journey and not as an end. And I tend to make sure that I enjoy the journey.

    9   8   7   6   5   4   3   2   1
    Agree   *Disagree*

19. I often seek excellence, but I am not a superperfectionist.

    9   8   7   6   5   4   3   2   1
    Agree   *Disagree*

20. In business, I am a strategist, not simply a jungle fighter.

    9   8   7   6   5   4   3   2   1
    Agree   *Disagree*

21. I value quality infinitely more than quantity.

    9   8   7   6   5   4   3   2   1
    Agree   *Disagree*

22. I face the realities of life directly, and then work positively from that point on.

    9   8   7   6   5   4   3   2   1
    Agree   *Disagree*

How to Score Your Self-Test

Total all the circled numbers. If your total was between 176 and 198, you are well on your way to becoming a USP and an outstanding effective thinker. You are apparently enjoying a very high level of three-dimensional success in your life. You compare very favorably with the USPs of my study. This book will serve you as a buttress, supporting much of the thinking that you are currently doing.

If you scored between 95 and 175, you are currently in the middle range, the semi-successful group. Most people fall in this group. You will clearly benefit from learning more about effective thinking. But be careful, because a person in your position can go either up or down. Take time now, to review your responses on this self-test; pay particular attention to items where you scored 6 or less. Then as you progress through the four steps of the effective thinking process, be sure to give extra concentration to the portions that apply to those items.

Finally, if you scored 94 or less, you are in the lowest third. You are more than a bit self-defeating, especially when it comes to job satisfaction or personal life satisfaction. But don't be alarmed. Becoming an effective thinker and attaining three-dimensional success are still wide open to you. I think you will find it heartening to know that I have had many clients who scored similarly on this test, who by consistent application of effective thinking, were able to reverse their self-defeating ways with just a little help and practice.

Getting Ready to Learn

Now that you know what aspects of effective thinking you wish to concentrate on, the rest of this book will show how to learn the process, step by step. As I start out to teach you how to do effective thinking, I make three important assumptions about you.

   1. You are open to taking total self-responsibility. You are *open to learning* how to take 100 percent responsibility for the way you think, feel, and behave (if you are not now doing it).
   There is, as you can imagine, a good deal of resistance to this notion. It's much more convenient to blame other people or outside events. That's why I use the phrased "open to learn." I am assuming that you are *open to learning* how to take total responsibility—not just partial—for your thinking, your feelings, and your behavior. If you're willing to learn that, I'll show you how.
   In my study of USPs I found several common character traits: self-esteem, integrity, listening ability, and the capacity to make wise decisions. But their major quality was their willingness take 100 percent total self-responsibility. In fact, that is what enabled them to attain these other marvelous traits.
   It is important to note that USPs do not take total responsibility for things *outside* their direct control, only for things directly *within* their control.
   USP Brenda Kullen, a thirty-nine-year-old corporation president and head of a major marketing firm, discussed her negative feelings after being blocked for a promotion four years earlier.

   At first, I was sure that it was because I was a woman. I felt that there was tremendous prejudice against women, as they move higher and high up the corporate ladder. Initially, all I could do was blame the system for blocking my promotions. And I was angry. Very angry. And my anger was getting in the way of my work, no question about that.

So, it was then that I took charge. I stopped blaming the system and the male power structure for my anger. My anger was coming from me. Sure, the circumstances were not good, but my reaction to the circumstances was totally under my own control. I decided to take charge of my anger. I converted it into energy. I used it to make me work even harder and better. And I used it to look for a better opportunity. A year later, I came to my present company as a vice-president. And then when the opportunity presented itself, I threw my hat in the ring for CEO. And I made it.

2. *You are open to learning the difference between effective and defective thinking.* I am counting on you to concentrate and learn all you can about the very subtle but very important differences between effective thoughts and defective thoughts. Are you willing to put aside the common misunderstandings about thoughts? Are you willing to learn to distinguish an effective thought from a thought that seems effective but is really defective?

For example, you might think that having *reasonable* expectations about waiting in line at the motor vehicle department is an effective thought. But *realistic*—not merely reasonable—expectations are much more effective. It is *reasonable* to assume that the line will move at a steady pace, but it is *realistic* to recognize that such offices often have many delays. If you are realistic, you'll bring something interesting to read while you wait in line!

3. *You are open to learning how to choose effective thoughts.* Human beings are the only living creature with the

capacity to willfully choose their thoughts, instead of docilely accepting any thought that happens to pop into their head. Unfortunately, there is a very strong resistance to accepting the reality that as humans we are gifted with the capacity for "thought choosing."

This is the bottom line: *We humans, are fully responsible for the thoughts we choose and consequently for the feelings and actions that are produced by those thoughts.* Many people have either forgotten this important fact or never fully understood it.

Why are your thoughts so important? Because your thoughts produce *all* your feelings and *all* your meaningful behavior. As a human being you are composed only of thoughts, feelings, and behavior. Your thoughts are the key to your existence. Your feelings result from your thoughts. Feelings are important because that is where you really live your life—in the realm of feelings under your own skin. Behavior is simply the tip of the iceberg, the small part of you that goes public. So choosing your thoughts—*effective* thoughts—makes everything else fall into place.

Often people protest, "But what about all those thoughts that just come into my head? I didn't choose them, but there they are." USPs always reserve the right to decide whether to *entertain* any thought that just happens to "come to mind." As adults, you and I are fully responsible for whether we *honor* any of the thoughts that come into our awareness, even thoughts that we did not put there in the first place. If a thought that has come into the foreground of our conscious mind is not useful, we can, as a matter of free will, dismiss it and choose another thought to put in its place.

So. . . . Are we ready to begin? Can you answer "yes" to the following three assumptions?

Assumption 1:   I am open to learning more precisely how I can take 100 percent responsibility for

choosing my own thoughts and the feelings
and behavior that result.

Your answer: _____

Assumption 2: I am open to learning how I can become
proficient at differentiating between effective thoughts (for me) and defective thoughts
(for me).

Your answer: _____

Assumption 3: I remain open to learning more about how
to actively choose thoughts to help me deal
effectively with any situation, on or off the
job.

Your answer: _____

If you still feel a bit dubious about the power of effective
thinking, that is normal. Resistance to change is very natural,
especially change in something as personal as the way we do
our thinking. After all, we are all products of years of
conditioning. And I'm sure you've heard all kinds of prom-
ises about all sorts of "new" ideas—only to end up disappointed. But this approach will work, if you learn it and,
more important, if you apply it. USPs are living testimony
that the ET process works. If it works for them, it can work
for you too.

Chapter 2

Establish Your Success Goals

[Explains why it is important to firmly establish achieving uncommon success as your primary life goal, and shows how to do so. Once you have established uncommon success as your major goal, you have set the stage for successfully engaging the four-step effective thinking process. A series of exercises provides additional assistance in developing other personal and professional goals.]

In the previous chapter I briefly mentioned that all uncommonly successful people, without exception, share one fundamental goal: uncommon success. They are determined to have the best life possible, according to their own very personal definitions, and they expect to achieve that by striving for success in all three dimensions.

And you must do the same. Before you can ever fully use the four-step ET process, you must have your main lifetime goal clearly in mind, and that main goal must be "uncommon success." You may have other goals that are worthwhile and important (in fact, this chapter will help you establish them), but the one major commitment must be "uncommon success."

Why is it so critical that you be very clear about your lifetime goal *before* initiating the four-step ET Process? Because the very meaning of word *effective* is "getting the *results* you intended." And if you are not clear about the results (goal) you intend to get, then there is no way to determine whether your thinking is effective.

Goal-Setting Secrets of USPs

USPs know exactly what they are after: uncommon, three-dimensional success. Their passionate pursuit of this one goal is their hallmark. USPs are uncommonly successful, not by accident or amazing good luck, but by design. They are, in fact, almost obsessive about attaining and sustaining the high level of personal and professional success that they have come to enjoy.

In my study of USPs, I tired to learn as much as I could about their approach to goal setting. Some of their ideas may be helpful to you as you begin the process of establishing your own personal and professional goals.

• *Maintain focus on the main goals.* USPs know exactly what they are after. Like most of us, they have a number of special goals and ambitions: making a good living, sustaining important relationships, seeing the world, enjoying good health, making a contribution to the world, perhaps obtaining certain material possessions.

You could wake up any USP at 3:00 A.M. and ask her, "What are your professional goals?" And she could tell you: one, two, and three. You could ask, "What are your personal goals?" and she could enumerate them too—one, two, and three.

But to USPs these are merely subgoals; they rest firmly on the foundation of one all-encompassing, overriding goal: uncommon success, personally and professionally. USPs phrase their pursuit of uncommon success in their own language, but it all boils down to: "a highly satisfying personal and professional life—and if at all possible, not at the expense of any other person." And that is exactly what they achieve.

And because high satisfaction is a matter of attitude (effective thinking) and requires absolutely nothing from anyone else, they can achieve it without harming others.

USP Linda Adams, a thirty-six-year-old corporation lawyer from Ohio, has set her sights upon a high-quality life: "My life these days is moving very rapidly. But I try to take it slow and easy; I'm in no rush to get anywhere. For me, the good life is quality over quantity. Quality in terms of my relationships. Quality in terms of work that I do. Quality in terms of my entire life. Life is much too short and important to waste running around in circles."

▪ *A goal must be something you can achieve entirely by thinking.* Be sure that any goals you set are goals you can surely achieve. The only goals that a USP takes seriously are goals that can be independently achieved by thought choosing alone, and nothing else—*because those are the only ones that are truly under their control.* USPs concentrate on goals they can be sure to achieve. Once they achieve them, they set new goals—often difficult and challenging, but always achievable.

▪ *Be careful what you set your sights on.* USPs are very careful what they go after in life, because they know they are likely to get it.

▪ *Happiness is a by-product, not the goal.* There is a great distinction between a rich and satisfying life and a happy life. USP Ted Owens, a sixty-three-year-old chemist who recently changed jobs, talks about happiness. "It's like chasing a butterfly. Chase after it and it is very difficult to catch. But get your mind on something else, perhaps helping another person, or concentrating on a project, or working in the garden, and lo and behold, often that same butterly comes over and lands on your shoulder. After all these years, I've come to realize that happiness makes for a better by-product than an end. Aiming for just happiness does not serve me very well as a life goal."

Pursuing happiness has nowhere near the payoff that the pursuit of life satisfaction has. Happiness is best pursued indirectly, by directly pursuing life satisfaction. Life satisfaction is readily achievable through effective thinking.

▪ *Contentment is not the goal either.* In fact, contentment is a dead end. USPs want a great deal of satisfaction but they never want to be *completely* satisfied. They value yearning, moving, working toward a goal. They do excellent work, and they have an excellent personal life, but they are not perfectly satisfied with either. They always want to improve. It is the striving to do just a little bit better that adds to their general life satisfaction. "If I ever end up totally satisfied with something—then it's over for me," said one USP. And I don't want things to be over, at least not yet."

▪ *The goal is not to cope, but to be an active agent of change.* While USPs know better than most how to make the best out of a given situation, they are not mere observers of the passing scene. They face the realities of a given situation, but they also do everything humanly possible to institute necessary change.

▪ *Aim high.* Because USPs are change agents, they are willing to take the necessary risks to pursue their dreams. They are not afraid to aim high, and they are not afraid to lose.

USP Vera Charles, a thirty-nine-year-old corporation president, says, "I set my standards extremely high when it comes to the quality of this life of mine because it's the one goal, I'm sure I can realize, since it's *my* standard I have to meet. I know that I may not really come in first in terms of life quality, but who can really measure that anyhow? But by aiming so high, I tend to do better than if I aimed for less."

Establishing Your Individual Goals

So far we've been talking about the fundamental goal of all USPs: uncommon success, the foundation on which all other goals rest. We discovered that there are subtle shades of understanding that can be useful as you make the commitment to yourself that uncommon success will be your lifelong goal.

Having made that commitment, you are ready to evaluate specific personal and professional goals, and establish your individual "package." You might begin by asking yourself this question: What is your definition of success?

Of course there's the obvious material success that comes with having plenty of money. And there is fame, and all its attendant material benefits. But there is also another kind of success, success grounded in attitudes, that can be achieved even without fame and fortune. This is the uncommon success that is readily attained by USPs.

For all too many of those who have only material success, life has proved to be unfulfilling. Many live with a pervasive fear that their possessions will be snatched away. They seem to be prisoners of their own possessions.

This leads to the first of several recommendations you might bear in mind as you go about setting your own goals.

• *Remind yourself that material goals will prove to be empty over time.* In my practice as a therapist, I have seen many people who would be considered successful by conventional standards—and who are actually miserable. The more of them I see, the more I have come to appreciate that the trappings of everyday success are just that—traps.

The issue here is not whether it is good or bad to have money. Obviously it's a good thing to have *some*. The question is, how much? How much is enough? And that is fundamentally a question of attitude. Which is why I say that the head of a major corporation, a Nobel prize winner, a famous athlete, or a rock star may have the trappings of success and still not be nearly as successful as a USP.

• *Beware that your goals are not just "fool's gold."* Be sure that what you aim for is what you really want. Do the necessary research and check—firsthand, if possible—to see if what you have set your sights on makes sense.

Arlene Fredericks, a computer programmer, wanted more than anything else to get promoted. So she worked long and hard, and one day she got exactly what she thought she wanted. Before long she realized that the "job of her dreams" was not at all like she had imagined it would be. Arlene would have been wise to do a "validity check" on her aspirations. She could have interviewed someone who had that job, or perhaps tried it out part time.

Before you set your mind on a goal, ask yourself very directly, "Is that what I really want for myself?" And then ask yourself the second important question: "Why?" You may be pursuing a goal for the wrong reason. Perhaps you want to prove something to your parents, or your boss. But what about you? Ask yourself, "What do I want for *me*?"

In your personal life, too, try to avoid chasing goals that don't make sense. How many people do you know who pinned their hopes for happiness on meeting and marrying Mr. or Ms. Right, only to find that they still felt the same void even when they did?

Once you have your major goal—uncommon success—under your direct command, other goals become less important—and paradoxically easier to achieve. Because you no longer desperately *need* that job promotion to enjoy your life, it more readily comes your way. You don't *need* a new car to feel better about yourself—and that too becomes easier to get, simply because you took the pressure off yourself.

▪ *Make sure that your goal does not depend primarily on events that are out of your direct control.* Be sure that what you seek (in a serious way) is not dependent on what others think of you, or on events that are outside of your control. Often this means designating the goal as a preference (rather than a need) and rephrasing it. For example, if one of your job-satisfaction goals requires that you be promoted, you might be better off to restate this goal: "To become fully qualified to be promoted" or perhaps, "to do, on a voluntary basis, a particular job that normally occurs only with promotion." Now you have a goal that you can accomplish, because the power to do it remains entirely in your own hands.

Perhaps one of your goals is to speak more distinctly, or to improve your computer skills. Those undertakings are entirely up to you. The power for doing them resides within you: motivation and hard work. In fact, these goals are entirely dependent upon whether your thinking is effective.

If any of your life-satisfaction goals are primarily dependent on outside circumstance, the opinions of others, or very good luck, it is all right to have them, but please don't take them too seriously. Keep a sense of humor about them.

Using rephrasing, it is also possible to design almost any goal so that you successfully achieve it within your time frame. And it's important to do so, because that way you will make goal achievement a habit.

If you set a specific date for achieving a goal, be sure that those dates are realistic. Suppose you decided that you want to be the president of your company in two years. Is that realistic? Many things could happen over the next two years, and some of them are out of your control.

If you insist on a time frame, then consider describing your same ambition in a slightly different way, perhaps: "I aim to be fully qualified to be president of this company in the next two years." Becoming qualified is up to you; being selected is up to others, even fate. By doing this kind of phrasing, you can make goal realization a habit. And success, of course, breed success.

As a side note, most goals of USPs have no serious deadlines connected with them. If a USP wants to write a book, you can be sure she'll write it, no matter how long it takes her. If a USP wants to start a new business, you can be sure that the new business will be started, no matter how long it takes.

• *Review your goals regularly.* Because times change and you change too, it is wise to review your personal and professional goals periodically, especially if you're involved in major life-changing events, such as a new job, a new marriage, or a new home. But even then, it is essential to remind yourself that uncommon success is still your number-one passion, your obsession.

• *Give yourself the benefit of the doubt.* It is easy to believe that uncommon success is achievable for other people—but not you. Some of my clients have said, in essence, "Well, maybe such a life is possible for some people, but they didn't have my history (my mother, my maladies, my brother, my boss)." During effective thinking seminars I often ask the participants to cover their eyes and raise their hands if they think it's a little more difficult for them to have a very high level of existence than the others in the room. When they open their eyes, they usually see that almost *everyone* has a hand raised!

Goal-Setting Exercises

Many people have difficulty coming to grips with what they want from life. For a variety of reasons having to do with psychology and human nature, they resist doing the work of weighing their values and establishing goals. Because this is true, I have developed a series of exercises to guide people painlessly (well, almost painlessly) through the process. If you will keep an open mind, and do a few of these exercises, I think you will find at the end that you have significantly clarified things for yourself.

There are eight exercises. It is not necessary to complete all eight in detail during your first reading; two or three may be sufficient. But look them all over and concentrate on the ones that strike your fancy. The only one that you absolutely *must* complete is Exercise 8. You can return to the others after you have learned more about the ET Process, if you wish. In fact, I recommend that you return to these eight exercises after you have completed your study of the entire ET Process, to recheck the validity of the personal and professional goals you set for yourself.

The main objective, at this point, is to thoroughly convince yourself that uncommon, three-dimensional success is your major goal. If you have any doubt, please actively read and do all seven exercises. Keep paper and pencil on hand; it's important that you commit to uncommon success in writing. But if you are quite certain that you are after three-dimensional success, then move directly to Exercise 8. In any case, be sure to complete Exercise 8 by signing it on the bottom line before you leave this chapter.

GOAL-SETTING EXERCISE 1 (Part A)

What If You Had Only One Year Left to Live?

Imagine that you have just left your physician's office. The doctor has just informed you that you will definitely have, at best, only one year left to live. You will not be in any pain, but you have only 365 days left." In the next 365 days, what three things would you be sure to do? List them below, in priority order.

1. _____
   _____
   _____

2. _____
   _____
   _____

3. _____
   _____
   _____

Next, take this exercise a step forward. Assume that eleven months have passed and you have procrastinated (denial, even in the face of overwhelming evidence, is not uncommon). Your physician tells you that you have only thirty days left to live. *Now,* what three things would you do?

1. _____
   _____
   _____

2. _____
_____
_____

3. _____
_____
_____

With only thirty days left, are any of your actions different?

1. _____
_____
_____

2. _____
_____
_____

3. _____
_____
_____

Finally, you reach the point where you have only 48 hours left to live. List the three things that you would do. Is anything different?

1. _____
_____
_____

2. _____

   _____

   _____

3. _____

   _____

   _____

  I have often asked participants to complete this exercise
as part of effective thinking seminars. Most people list such
things as "getting my affairs in order," "travel," and "getting together and sharing with my loved ones."
  We then discuss the question of when. *When* are you
going to begin doing these things that are so important to
you? Review your own responses. If you identified one or
two things that are very important to you and you are not
currently doing them, I would ask you the same question:
When are you going to begin?

GOAL-SETTING EXERCISE 1 (Part B)

Do You Have a Special Sense of Mission in Your Life?

As a finale to this goal-clarifying exercise, imagine that you are taking a walk on a beautiful green grassy knoll. It is a very beautiful day. The air is fresh. The sky is a bright blue and there are many white fleecy clouds. You are feeling very good. Things are going well.

Then off to your right you spot a white object at the edge of the horizon and you walk over to it. As you get closer to it you realize that it is a marble tombstone. When you reach it, you see, to your astonishment, that it reads "Here lies [Your Name]." Under your name is an epitaph.

Pause and reflect for a moment. If you could create an epitaph that described what you really wanted out of your life, what would it say? What would you like to be remembered for?

My epitaph: I would like to be remembered as follows:

_____

_____

_____

_____

Of course, the good news is that you are not dead yet. If you are not doing very much these days to live up to your epitaph, it's time now to move to into action.

GOAL-SETTING EXERCISE 2

"I'm Sorry That . . ."

Imagine that is ten years later than it is right now. You and everyone you know are ten years older; prices are higher. But, for the sake of this exercise nothing else has really changed in your life; over the past ten years, your life has been more or less at a standstill. You never did all of those exciting things that you intended to do. Your career has remained at a standstill. You never wrote that book, never earned that degree, you never took that dream vacation. Then after you run through all the things that you didn't do, *stop*. Now complete each of the following sentences:

I'm sorry that I never _____
_____
_____

I'm sorry that I never _____
_____
_____

I'm sorry that I never _____
_____
_____

I'm sorry that I never _____
_____
_____

Of course it's not really ten years later; it's still now. You have many years ahead of you. Ask yourself: Am I actively moving toward accomplishing the things I listed? If not, what are you waiting for?

GOAL-SETTING EXERCISE 3

Urgent Goals vs. Urgent and Important Goals

Make two separate lists of goals. Label one "urgent goals" and the other "urgent *and* important goals." Urgent goals are what we require to survive or just get by in life. Minor urgencies include returning important phone calls, filling out tax forms, and meeting deadlines. Major urgencies include dealing with illness, appearing for interviews, closing on a house, or making a sale. Urgent *important* goals might not occur to you at first. But USPs would place such divergent goals as "having a satisfying life" and "pursuing a life-long interest" under this category.

Just be certain that everything on your "urgent *and* important" list is stated in a way that it can be achieved by thinking, rather than being dependent on outside events or the behavior of others. And you want to establish goals that are realistically achievable, and not just a matter of good luck.

To overcome any tendency to procrastinate, tell yourself that you won't have to do whatever it is for very long. Agree that you will do it for five minutes only, then stop. You may end up with more momentum than you can imagine.

GOAL-SETTING EXERCISE 4

Your Personal and Professional Lifeline

This exercise is designed to give you a different perspective on the way you have been living your life so far. Most lives are like the stock market, with various ups and downs but a general trend that, when viewed at a distance, can give useful insights about the direction your life is taking. If the direction in which you are moving makes sense, then you can stay the course. And if it isn't, a slight change may be all you need.

Step 1. On a separate sheet of paper, draw a diagonal line from the lower left-hand corner to the upper right-hand corner.

Step 2. Write your present age in the upper right-hand corner and the number 1 in the lower left-hand corner, indicating the beginning of your life.

Step 3. Divide your lifeline in half, noting half your present age at the midpoint (see Figure 2-1).

Step 4. Now recall one of the earliest experiences in your life that you can remember. It need not be critical, just something that you happen to remember as you are doing this. Mark on the line approximately when it occurred and, in your own shorthand, what it was.

Step 5. Take another seven or eight minutes and continue to move up the line, adding experiences that come to mind, up to your present age. (See Figure 2-2.) These experiences can be either positive or negative, and they need not be important to anyone else.

Step 6. Now look over your lifeline and review briefly the events that you happened to recall. (Remember, if you were to do this on a different day, the memories might have been a bit different.)

Figure 2-1. Your personal/professional lifeline.

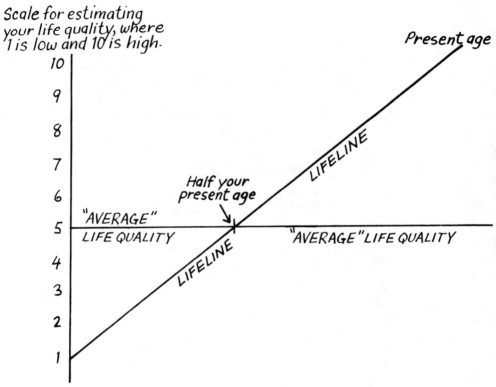

Step 7. Looking over your life, right now, give it a *title* as if you were naming a book or a movie. Your title can be original, or you might borrow one, perhaps "Gone With the Wind," "The Joys of Living," or "The Agony and the Ecstasy." Write your title over the top of your lifeline.

Step 8. In most lives there are a number of transition points. For example, if your childhood was very comfortable and pleasant but then you had a very difficult time in high school, you would have had a turning point. Starting a brand new career is another turning point. Locate a few of these in your life and draw a light vertical line at the appropriate point

Figure 2-2. Jack Smith's (age 40) personal/professional lifeline, after completing step 5.

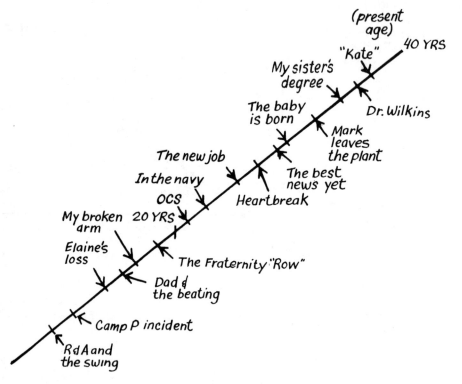

on your lifeline. Jot a descriptive phrase at each of these periods: "teenage misery," "changed to architecture." (See Figure 2-3.)

Step 9. Contemplate your lifeline once again. Look at the title that you selected and your transition points. Looking at your life from this perspective may offer you some interesting new insights. Write down some of your general observations about your life as you see it right now.

_____

_____

_____

_____

_____

Figure 2-3. Jack Smith's personal/professional lifeline, after completing step 8.

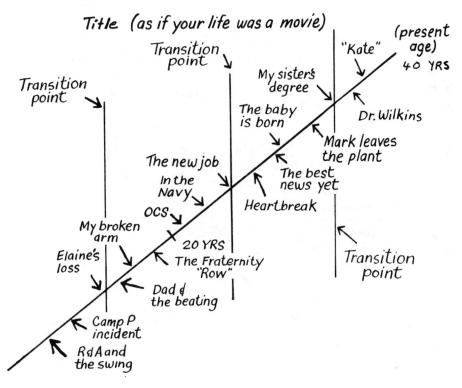

Title (as if your life was a movie)

Transition point

Transition point

"Kate"

(present age)
40 YRS

My sister's degree

The baby is born

Dr. Wilkins

Mark leaves the plant

The new job

In the Navy

The best news yet

OCS

Heartbreak

My broken arm

20 YRS

Elaine's loss

The Fraternity "Row"

Transition point

Dad & the beating

Camp P incident

R & A and the swing

Step 10. Lightly draw a horizontal line through the middle of your page. On the left hand-side of the paper, starting at the top, write the numbers 10 to 1; 5 should fall at the halfway point. Using this scale, where 1 is low and 10 is high, chart the general quality of your life satisfaction over the years. (On my example, I used a heavy dashed line.) The line will probably look like a stock market chart, with a series of ups and downs.

Step 11. Now stop and look at all that you have done in your lifeline. (Compare it to the completed lifeline of Jack Smith in Figure 2-4.) Here are some interesting things to look for.

1. Looking at your life, as you see it now, who (other than

Figure 2-4. Jack Smith's completed personal/professional lifeline.

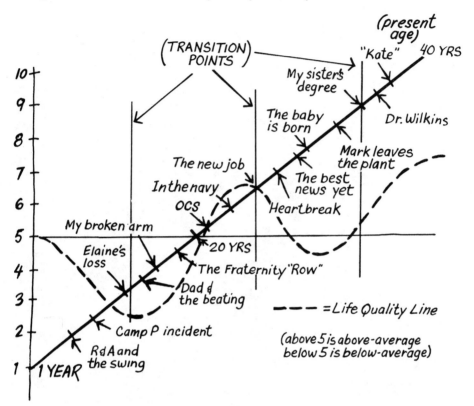

your spouse or parents) has been the most influential person? Put that person's name or initials somewhere on your lifeline. Is it possible that you could write or phone this person and thank him or her?

2. What do you recall as one of the loneliest times ever? Make a note of that on your lifeline. Many USPs have made important personal discoveries during lonely times: "I, alone, can choose any attitude that I want to."

3. What was one of the best times you ever had? Note that as well. This is probably an indication of what really gives you genuine pleasure.

4. What was one of the most significant events in your life

thus far? Did you think it was significant when it was happening?

The point of creating this lifeline is to give a fresh perspective about yourself. It is an opportunity to reflect on the direction and quality of your life thus far. Where you have been? Where you are going? Once you know where you want to go, you are ready—and that is step one.

GOAL-SETTING EXERCISE 5

Preferences vs. Needs

Finish the following sentence any way that comes to mind.
Then after you have completed a list of wants, place a *p* near
those that you prefer and an *n* next to those that you absolutely
need. I recommend that you place an *n* next to those that you
can be absolutely sure that you can have, by using effective
thinking. All others should be preferences. Remember, USPs
have many preferences but very few needs.

Out of my life, I want: _____

_____

_____

_____

_____

_____

_____

_____

_____

_____

_____

_____

GOAL-SETTING EXERCISE 6 (Part A)

Who Are You, Really?

This exercise is about defining yourself, instead of trying to "find yourself." It will provide you with a shortcut method for attaining in one fell swoop the USP attributes we introduced in Chapter 1: inner peace, a sense of purpose, and plenty of fun and adventure in life.

To complete the second part of this exercise you will need a tape recorder. Then, after you have a friend or associate record the tape from the script that I've provided, you'll need a quiet place to listen to it. Of course, this kind of activity may not suit everyone. But if you take the trouble to have the tape recording made as prescribed and then the willingness to really concentrate and follow the tape recorded instructions, it will work wonders for you. Participants in my workshops often say that this activity has made a genuine difference in the way they see themselves. The exercise is designed to help you to find an identity that has calm, purpose, and adventure plugged into it.

Now I am going to ask you one question several times: "Who are you?" But each time I ask the question, I will vary the emphasis just a bit. Your job is to give a different answer each time. I'll start with your name. Please give it. Then I'll move onto job and family, then beyond that. I think that you will find out something very interesting about your real identity as you go through this exercise.

Question	*Answer*
Who are you? [*Answer with your name, please.*]	I am _____
Who are you really? [*This time answer with your job title.*]	I am _____

Question	*Answer*
That's what you do, but who are you? [*Now answer with one or more of your family roles*—a mother, father, husband, wife, sister, son, daughter.]	I am _____
But that is not who you are either. That's just a role, a function. Who are you, please? [*Now say, "Me."*]	I am _____
Of course you are you. But that doesn't say anything. Who are "you?" You are certainly more than just a "me." [*Now answer the question any way you would like, but different from any answer that you gave before.*]	I am _____
Yes, I know what you said, but who is the real you? [*Answer differently again, in your own way.*]	I am _____
Yes, of course. But *who* are you?	I am _____
Sure. But who *are* you?	I am _____

Most people who go through with this exercise are left with an uneasy feeling. That's because most of us don't have a very clear picture of who we really are. We often get our identity from organizations or groups. But USPs are selective joiners, and they get their primary sense of identity from their own inner self-picture. Every USP has an inner identity that is not predicated on job title or family role, because neither of these is totally under the USP's direct control. USP Frank Saunders, president of Mayfair Airlines, says:

> My job as president of this company is largely under the control of my board of directors, and the fact that we have a healthy economy. I feel that my identity is much too important to put up for grabs to variables out of my control such as my board of directors or the national economy. My inner identity even goes beyond being Frank Saunders, father, husband, or airline president. I like to keep control of the really important things in life and who I am is one of the most important things of all in my life.''

If who you are embraces the life-enriching qualities of calm, purpose, and adventure, you will have an identity that has some very high payoff. And since you, and only you, can define yourself, why not define yourself in such a way that these three qualities are structured into the identity that you give yourself?

GOAL-SETTING EXERCISE 6 (Part B)

Accessing Your Hidden Identity

Have a friend or associate read the following script into a tape recorder and then play it back to yourself periodically. Find a quiet and comfortable place where you can concentrate without interruption for about five or six minutes. That's all that it will take for you to listen to the tape.

The script will suggest that in your mind's eye you visit a place of great beauty. There you will first experience a sense of great inner calm, then a sense of purposefulness, and finally a sense of adventure. Then you will experience all three ingredients at the same time, and at that point you will be asked to name this experience as if you were naming a vacation retreat, a summer home, or a boat. Then you will engrave this memory into your conscious mind and slowly open your eyes. The name and picture that you created will become, if you want it to, your hidden identity.

Here's the script; read it into your tape recorder.

Please shut your eyes. Now listen carefully and follow the instructions and suggestions that I give you. Shut your eyes even tighter. Tighter still. Now let the little muscles on your eyelids relax. Now make your forehead very tense and very tight. Now relax your forehead. Let all the muscles in your forehead relax. Now become aware of the back of your neck. Be aware of all the tension that may have accumulated there, in the back of your neck. Now let the back of your neck relax, completely. Now be aware of your upper and lower jaws. Be aware of any tension there and now let your upper and lower jaws separate ever so slightly. Let your jaws relax.

Now do the same for your right arm and shoulder. Be very much aware of tension in your right arm and shoulder, and now let your shoulder and right arm relax completely. That's fine. That's very, very good. And now your left arm and shoulder. Make your left arm and shoulder very tight and very tense. Now let your left arm and shoulder relax.

Now as you breathe in, imagine that you are breathing in airs of relaxation and then as you breathe out, that you are breathing out all tension in your system. Breathing in, very slowly, airs of relaxation. As you breathe out, airs of tension out. [*Pause.*] Good.

Now in your mind's eye, visit your spinal column. As you know, your spinal column is connected to your entire nervous system. Now make your spinal column tense and tight for a moment. That's right, tension in your spinal column. Now let your entire spinal column relax. Let your entire spinal column relax. Very good. And now your whole nervous system is relaxing. Breathing in very slowly airs of relaxation and exhaling any remaining tension that you might still have. [*Pause.*] Now be aware of your right leg. Make it tense and tight. Good. Now let your right leg relax completely. Let it get tired and limp. And now your left leg. Be aware of your left leg. Make it tense and tight. And now let your left leg relax completely. Now you are very, very relaxed. [*Pause.*]

Now imagine that you are on a very comfortable elevator, and you are sitting in a very comfortable chair on that elevator. You can decide now whether you want the elevator to go up, or if you want the elevator to go down. Decide now, if you prefer to go up or down on the elevator. [*Pause.*] Fine, the elevator is going to go in that direction. Now I am going to count backwards from ten to one and with each number the elevator is going to take you progressively closer to a place of great beauty. A place of fantastic, exquisite beauty. Ready now. Ten. The elevator is moving you along and you are feeling very, very comfortable and relaxed. Moving along toward a place of great beauty. Nine. Moving along more and more. Very relaxed. Very comfortable. The elevator is taking you to a wonderful place of great beauty.

Eight. Very comfortable. Very, very relaxed. You haven't been this comfortable, this mellow in a very long time. Four. Moving along very comfortable, very relaxed. [*Pause.*] Seven. Moving along to a place of great beauty. You are doing very well. [*Pause.*] You are moving closer and closer to your destination, a place of utterly fantastic beauty. Six. The elevator is continuing to move you along and you are feeling very, very comfortable and relaxed. Moving along toward a place of great beauty.

Five. Moving along more and more. Very relaxed. Very comfortable. The elevator is taking you to a wonderful place of great beauty. Four. Very comfortable. Very, very relaxed. You haven't been this comfortable, this much at ease in a very long time. Three. Moving along very comfortable, very relaxed. [*Pause.*] Two. Moving along now and getting very, very close to your destination. Very close to your place of great beauty. You are doing very well. [*Pause.*] You are moving closer and closer to your destination, a place of utterly fantastic, great beauty.

And now, at last, one. You have arrived at your destination and the elevator door opens and there it is—a place of absolutely fantastic, gorgeous, marvelous beauty. You move effortlessly out of the elevator into this marvelous, beautiful, tranquil place. Now take it all in. Smell it. Taste it. Feel it. Experience it in your own way with all of your sense for the next twenty seconds. [*Pause for about twenty seconds.*]

Now you are experiencing a great sense of inner peace. Of inner tranquillity. Of inner calm. Experience your sense of inner calm in your own way for the next twenty seconds or so. [*Pause for about twenty more seconds.*]

Now, off in the distance, you sense something wonderful, something very important and wonderful going on, but you are not all that clear about what it is. All you know is that you are needed there. So now you find yourself moving effortlessly toward this other wonderful place off in the distance. You sense that it is important that you go there. Now pause for an additional twenty seconds or so and visit your sense of purpose. [*Pause for about twenty seconds.*] You have a great sense of importance. A feeling of mission—off in the distance, where you are needed.

And now experience the sense of adventure as you calmly, effortlessly are moving forward on your mission. Experience a sense of exhilaration and excitement combined with your inner calm and sense of purpose. Experience your sense of adventure, in your own way over the next twenty seconds. [*Pause again, for about twenty seconds.*]

Now you are experiencing a great sense of inner calm, combined with a great sense of purpose, combined with a great sense of adventure. Experience now the combination of calm, purpose, and adventure all at once. Calm, purpose, and adventure. Experience yourself this way for the next minute. In your own way. [*Pause now for about sixty seconds.*]

You have just experienced yourself at your innermost level. Now give this experience of yours a name, as if you are naming a vacation retreat, a summer home, or a ship. Perhaps an exotic or mysterious name. Whatever names comes to you just now. [*Pause.*] Now repeat that name that you have just come up with. Now repeat that name to yourself, slowly, three more times. This name is you—at the inner-self level. You will remember this name and be able to use it any time you want to remind yourself to be calmer, more purposeful, and more adventurous.

Okay, now answer these questions. Who are you? (Now repeat the name of your hidden identity.) Yes, but who are you really? (Same name). Yes, I know what you have said. But who is the real you. (Same name).

You will remember everything that you have done during this exercise. You will remember your hidden identity and be able to use it any time you want to. It can be one of your most valuable effective thoughts. Now in a moment, I am going to ask you to open your eyes and then you will pause and remind yourself of this entire experience. One. You are now feeling very refreshed. Two. Sit up in your chair now. Three. Now open your eyes. You are feeling very refreshed and very calm.

Now turn your tape recorder off and take some time for reflection. Then answer the following in the spaces provided.

Question 1. Who are you? [*Write the name that came to mind during this exercise, in the space below*].

My hidden identity name is: _____

For each of us, this exercise will produce something a bit different. If you are not entirely satisfied with the picture or name that rose up from your own subconscious, you can do it again, whenever you choose to. It is important, if you are to master the effective thinking process, that you access an identity that has calm, purpose, and adventure structured within it.

For example, one person came to the name Mellow Tourist. She explained, "My inner calm came from walking about as tourist, unencumbered with ordinary day-to-day problems. Each turn was a surprise. That was my sense of adventure. And my purpose, I suppose, came from having a general itinerary for my journey. I was going somewhere, even while I stopped to take in the sights."

Some of the hidden identity names that others discovered include Mountain High, Valhalla, Harmony, My Secret Place, Gentle Flowing Brook (mine), Daybreak on the Beach, Easy Passage, Soaring Eagle, Open Sky, Gliding Light, and many others derived from nature. Even names such as Rolling Rolls Royce, Prospering Executive, and CEO in Charge of Myself proved extremely helpful to certain people.

To further examine your experience with this exercise, please answer two more questions.

Question 2. What did you experience when you were moving forward effortlessly with a sense of purpose?

Answer: _____

_____

Question 3. How, exactly, did you feel when you combined calm, purpose, and adventure?

Answer: _____

_____

_____

GOAL-SETTING EXERCISE 7

Completing the following exercise is essential. After each sentence fragment, write whatever comes to mind. Your first impulse might very well be the most significant. This exercise, in essence, asks you to have a genuine commitment to the three-dimensional success lifestyle of uncommonly successful people.

High Performance on My Job

One of the high standards regarding the work that I do is:

_____

_____

Other high standards I have in the quality of the work that I do are:

_____

_____

_____

_____

_____

A High Level of Personal Life Satisfaction

I get great satisfaction in my personal life when I do the following:

_____

_____

_____

_____

_____

A High Level of Professional Life Satisfaction

I get great satisfaction in my work when I do the following:

_____

_____

_____

_____

_____

_____

_____

_____

_____

At this point, if your commitment to uncommon success is weak or uncertain, I recommend that you go back and repeat all the preceding exercises. It will be impossible for you to properly engage the four-step ET process if you do not have a clear, (even passionate) desire point to attain your own high level of uncommon success.

GOAL-SETTING EXERCISE 8

A Very Important Last Step

As the final step in goal setting, please initial the following sentence—but only if you can agree to subscribe to it.

> I have a strong desire to make the remainder of my life uncommonly successful. I want to be high achiever at the work that I do for a living. I want to genuinely enjoy my work, even in difficult times. And I want to have a very rich and satisfying personal life, even when things are difficult in that aspect of my life as well. In addition, I hope to have and sustain this uncommon success, not at the expense of any other person, if at all possible.
>
> [*Signed*] _____

Chapter 3

Effective Thinking, Step 1: Take Notice

[Explains why it's important to take notice of those times when you are not moving toward your goal of achieving uncommon success. Gives specific means for taking notice and monitoring your progress toward your goals. Provides five important questions and recommends answers. Introduces the life-quality game.]

The first step in the effective thinking process is willfully to "take notice." But what does that mean, exactly? What do you take notice of? Simply notice whether you are moving toward your goal of uncommon success. If you are, then just keep doing whatever you are doing. But if you notice that you are not moving along toward your goal, then you move on to the next step in the process.

You should do this periodically, as often as five or six times a day. It takes only a few seconds to do. And if you notice early enough, you can nip problems in the bud.

Taking notice means taking a brief inventory of your mental and physical state. Simply monitor your feelings, as you proceed with whatever you're doing. Try to sense what you are experiencing viscerally, in the pit of your stomach, in the back of your neck, in your jaws, in your head. Check out what you are feeling in your heart, in your spine, in your throat, behind your eyes.

The ET Process for Uncommon Success

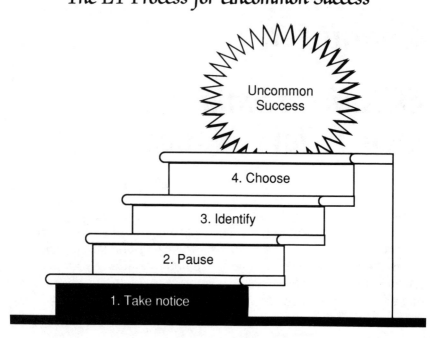

Step 1: Take Notice

Suppose one of your colleagues is speaking in a loud, abrasive way. In this context "take notice" means that you notice that his way of talking is upsetting you. Then ask yourself, "Is my getting upset in concert with the uncommon success goal that I have set for myself?" If it is, do nothing. But if it isn't—and it is likely that getting upset is adding nothing to your life—then go to step 2. If your job satisfaction level is being lowered by your colleague's loud and abrasive ways, then you are being diverted from three-dimensional success.

It's important to learn to sense the little things that can affect your progress toward your goal. In fact, it's often the bothersome details that can spoil the quality of your life and defeat your pursuit of uncommon success.

Of course even more troublesome things can most certainly keep you from your success goals: a difficult boss, unfairness on the job, a sick child, deadline stress, or very serious obstacles such as getting fired, having your assignment taken from you, or a major accident.

Here are some obvious questions you might ask yourself periodically as part of your goal monitoring:

"Am I really living the life of someone who is uncommonly successful?"

"Am I really enjoying this?"

"*Should* I be enjoying [listening to this person talking to me just now/reading this poorly written report/paying attention at this awful meeting/trying to ski down this godforsaken mountain]?"

USPs do not have to enjoy every minute of their lives. But every minute (or almost every minute) should be moving them toward uncommon success, either directly or indirectly. Suffering through a poorly written report, for example, can be directly worthwhile if the report contains useful information. It may be indirectly worthwhile if your boss asked you to read it and you need to please your boss to keep your job and keeping your job provides you with income to travel and traveling is one of your important goals.

Things that are worthwhile (directly or indirectly) must be done. But it is not necessary to get yourself upset while doing them, and that is where steps 2, 3, and 4 of the effective thinking process come into play.

Five Monitoring Questions

Periodically—at least twice a day, in the beginning—ask yourself these five basic goal-monitoring questions:

1. Who am I with?
2. Why am I?
3. Where am I?
4. When am I?
5. How am I?

Basic Question Number 1—Who Am I With?
Recommended Answer: My Hidden Identity.

One of the most important questions you will ever ask yourself is "Who am I?" And of you answer with your hidden identity (see exercise number 6 in Chapter 2), you'll automatically remind yourself about calm, purpose, and adventure. Ask yourself this question the next time your ego seems to be taking a beating.

Since you are always in your own company, be sure to remind yourself that you are a person well worth being with. Remind yourself that you *are* your hidden identity—a person who deserves a life filled with inner calm, a sense of purpose, and plenty of adventure. Let's check these out, one at a time.

Inner Calm

Monitor your present level of inner calm. If you have a very tense stomach and cold, sweaty palms, you may be suffering from a lack of sufficient inner peace. Then you can use the next steps of the effective thinking process to remind yourself of how worthwhile you really are.

Purpose

Periodically, ask yourself, "Am I living a life that is meaningful?"

I have asked many people in my seminars what it was that gave them a sense of purpose in life. Most answers seem to fall into two basic categories: "Having someone or something to care for that goes beyond myself," and "accomplishing something worthwhile, something that is very important."

Sometimes an important project can make your life more meaningful. USPs always seem to have "a big project" of one kind or another underway: writing a novel, doing volunteer work, helping a sick friend, doing a special project on the job, earning an advanced degree. USPs insist, however, that the success of their project be judged completely on their own terms. USPs do not seriously accept external deadlines that force them to compromise the standards of quality that they set for themselves. It may take them a year to do what another person can do in a month, but that doesn't deter the USP in the slightest.

Adventure

Ask yourself periodically if you are having enough fun in your life, enough excitement. If not, ask yourself if you're taking sufficient risks. Just make sure any risk you take is

completely in harmony with your other uncommon success
goals.

For example, USP Joe Smith was considering whether
he should take the risk of switching to a higher-paying job in
another section of the country. He evaluated the risk in light
of how it would affect inner peace and his sense of purpose.
He asked himself, "If I accept this job, what will that do to
my sense of inner calm, and does it tie in with my lfie
purposes? If changing jobs will have an unfavorable effect on
my wife and the rest of my family, I have to consider that.
They are my main reason for living. I can handle the excitement. In fact the whole idea is exhilarating to me. But I had
better have a long talk with my family first, before I make
this decision."

When you are facing a risk, ask yourself the following:

1. Is the risk worthwhile?
2. Can you imagine handling the situation if you were to
   fail?
3. Can you vividly picture yourself succeeding, in ideal
   fashion?
4. Can you enthusiastically go for it?

• *Step 1: Decide if the risk is worthwhile.* Detemine
whether the risk is in concert with your other life goals. Is
taking this risk going to interfere with your goal of achieving
inner peace? Is it in concert with the sense of purpose that
you are pursuing? If Joe Smith wants to change jobs at
midcareer, he had better first check out the realities of the
job market and make some realistic estimates of his chances
for success.

• *Step 2: Plan how you would handle the worst.* The
worst-case scenario is commonly recommended strategy for
preparing to take a business risk. What if Joe Smith failed at
the new job—could he handle that? This step in risk taking
isn't too difficult for USPs because they have many effective
thoughts in readiness to help them through any "failure" that
comes their way.

If Joe Smith figures out in advance exactly how he could endure failure, he can then move comfortably to risk-taking step 3. But if he skips this necessary step, the fear of failure will haunt him and keep him from making optimal decisions.

▪ *Step 3: Vividly picture yourself succeeding.* At this juncture, Joe Smith must ask himself if he can vividly picture himself succeeding. If, in his mind's eye he can see himself at work in the new setting, doing well, then he's ready for step 4. Olympic athletes report that they actually *see* themselves breaking world records, just before they do it. If you are about to jump from one point to another, use your imaginative powers to see yourself succeeding just before you do it.

▪ *Step 4: Do it.* Actually take that risk and go for it with vigor. Spontaneity becomes really important here. Joe Smith, if he got this far, is now in an excellent position to succeed. At this point, it is time to take the risk, and undertake it with gusto.

To summarize, as you move through life, reflect as you go: "Am I experiencing sufficient inner calm, a clear sense of purpose, and enough fun and adventure in my life?" If you are, you will notice that a special kind of synergy takes place. The calmer you get, the easier it is to clarify your purposes. And when your life's purposes are clear, and you feel calm inside, you will be in a better position to take more effective risks and consequently have more fun.

Basic Question Number 2: Why Am I?
Recommended Answer: *To Have a Great Life—That's Why I Am.*

That's a very deep and philosophical question—"Why are you?"— and USPs tend to keep their own answer relatively uncomplicated. USP Ben Richardson, a thirty-seven-year-pastor of a large Midwestern church, says, "I don't have the answers to the many mysteries of life, but I do have a sense of my personal mission. My mission is to have one of the best lives possible, in the short time allotted to me here.''

Basic Question Number 3: Where Am I?
Recommended Answer: *Here.*

Where you are currently is always ''here.'' You have been ''here'' all of your life. Consequently, if through effective thinking, you make your various ''here's'' uncommonly successful, you will have a rich and satisfying life. In the future, you will be ''here'' as well.

Basic Question Number 4: When Am I?
Recommended Answer: *Now.*

Your life is made up entirely of ''nows''—present moments. You past is simply ''nows'' used up, and your future is simply ''nows'' sent ahead. If you know how to make your nows rich and satisfying (through effective thinking) then your past will be excellent, your future bright, and your present moments fulfilling.

Basic Question Number 5: How Am I?
Recommended Answer: *The Best Is Yet to Come.*

The answer to this question, like the others, becomes a self-fulfilling prophecy. If you answer appropriately, you can stack the odds for your future in your favor.

   USPs answer the question a bit differently than most. Some people like to say, ''Great. Never felt better.'' Others are negative. ''Not too good. This (or that) hurts.'' But USPs answer the question in a way that sustains within them great hope for the future. Hope is a very important ingredient in making your present circumstances rich and satisfying. Say it to yourself right now: ''The best is yet to come.'' You may find that just saying it brings a smile to your face. It's true, of course. The best *is* yet to come. How do I know that? I don't, really. But if I believe it, I tend to stack the odds in that direction. Since there are no absolutes, especially about your future, why not stack the odds in your favor?

My father, who died a few years ago at age ninety, was a USP. He was a high-spirited person who worked very hard all his life, but also knew how to enjoy himself, both personally and professionally. My mother died when he was eighty-five. He grieved deeply, intensely, and respectfully—but only for about six months. Then after that, he remarried and took off with his lovely new wife for a Hawaiian honeymoon and another five good years of life. A week before he died, he happened to say, "Jerry, my boy, remember, the best is yet to come!"

Taking Notice Takes Practice

Because this first step is so uncommon, it takes practice before you can expect to do it as a matter of course. But you must do the practice, because you want to get to the point where taking notice is a habit.

USPs constantly practice by noticing when they hear statements like these:

"My work makes me feel [good/bad/tired]."
"This job would be OK if it weren't for the [customers/
   boss/politics] of this place."
"That SOB that works with me is driving me crazy."
"When my boss stands over my shoulder, he makes me
   nervous."
"The noise in the office is ruining my life."
"This daily commute to work is killing me."
"My [husband/wife/lover] is giving me an ulcer."
"Those deadly conversations at lunch bore the daylights
   out of me."

USPs know that all these statements are false. They are the result of *thinking*. USPs know that "outside circumstances" don't make people feel or act in particular way, but rather the "inside circumstances." And since USPs are in charge of their inside circumstances, and since suffering is not one of their goals, they take notice and see to it they don't continue to choose thoughts along those lines.

Play the Life-Quality Game

If you desire to have very high level of life satisfaction as your primary goal, the looking at life as a game is an interesting and useful way of measuring how you are doing.

The main objective of the game is to gather as many life quality points (LQPs) as possible in the time allotted. A life quality point is a unit of excellent life quality. In a single minute you can earn as many as ten units. The idea is to gather as many LQPs as possible in each minute of your life. If you suffer for no good reason in a given minute, you would get zero LQPs. If you suffer constructively (perhaps feeling the pain over the loss of a loved one but moving toward eventual acceptance of that loss) you would certainly get some LQPs even though you aren't having what could be described as a "good time." If you have a peak experience or a marvelous minute, you might earn as many as 10 LQPs for that minute. Again, the purpose of the game is to earn as many LQPs as is possible in the time allotted (your lifetime.)

On a scale from 1 to 10 (1 is low and 10 is high), rate the general quality level of your personal life over the last five years.

My rating of my personal life quality level over the past five years as I perceive it just now is about: ＿＿ .

Now rate your perceived level of the quality of your professional life over the past five years.

> The rating of my professional life quality as I perceive it over the past five years is about: _____ .

If your scores were high, you're off to a good start for playing the rest of the game. But even if they are not, you can be a winner. All you have to do, from this point on, is take notice of when you are scoring 5 or less and then do some new thinking to bring your minute-by-minute average up to a 7 or an 8 or even higher. USPs are experts at collecting a very high percentage of the LQPs available in any given minute.

People who take the life quality game seriously, armed with the know how of the effective thinking process, are at great advantage. Even if they should live a relatively short time, they can outperform a self-defeating person who lives many years longer. Winning this game (just as in real life) is matter of quality over quantity.

USPs, like all of us, have their ups and downs. But they try not to waste too much time in the life quality game being depressed or angry. USPs put a definite limit on the amount of time they are willing to suffer.

USPs take a two-pronged attack on difficulties: action plus attitude. For example, if you are finding that the politics in your workplace are getting you down and seem to be keeping you from getting your fair quota of LQPs, then it behooves you to attack that situation. Do what you can to improve company politics. But at the same time, while you are working on the issue, maintain an effective attitude. Collect LQPs even while the repair work is going on.

The principle holds true in personal life. If planning the family vacation is becoming stressful, be aware of what is happening to the quality of your life and do something about it. Use both action and attitude. Try some different techniques for making your plans, even silly ones. Put a map of the country on the wall and throw darts to pick your destinations; or put all your ideas on slips of paper and let the youngest member of the family, blindfolded, choose one. If it's a question of conflict over where to go, work out a weighted ranking system, and give everyone in the family scorecards. Or give each school-age child a research assignment: Go to the library and find out all you can about the national parks, every state that has a coastline, the vacation possibilities in every state that begins with the letter A. At the same time, work on your attitude: "No matter where we go, or what we do, we will have a rich and satisfying time."

Remember, each minute that goes by in which you didn't collect a maximum of LQPs will not go by again.

Once you have trained yourself to become keenly aware that you are serious player of the life quality game, you will quickly recognize when opportunities to gather points are passing you by. When that happens, it's time move immediately to step 2 of the effective thinking process.

Chapter 4

Effective Thinking, Step 2: Pause

[Explains why it is necessary that you pause. Describes the hypnotic power of a self-defeating mindset. Emphasizes the importance of compartmentalizing the problem and moving on with other areas of life. Provides practice exercise.]

Whenever you take notice that you are not moving toward your goal of uncommon success, it is time to pause. It doesn't matter whether you are clearly off track or only slightly off your goal, you still need to pause. If a particular person or situation is upsetting you, if you find that you are suffering too much, if you are a little too intense, or too nervous, or overly tired, it is time to take time out.

The main purpose of pausing is to create *a break in the self-defeating mindset that you are obviously in.* During the pause you institute measures to turn whatever "problem" you are facing into a very manageable "project." This is when you do all the detective work necessary to locate the defective thoughts and identify effective thoughts to replace them.

Prompt Yourself to Pause

One of the most obvious cues is to simply say to yourself, "Stop." Use any kind of wording that will command your

The ET Process for Uncommon Success

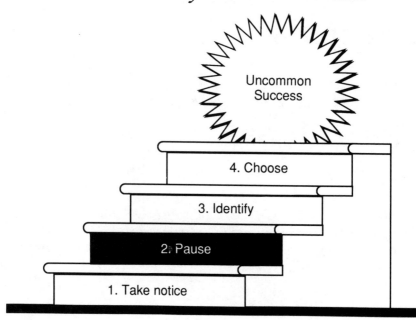

Step 2: Pause

full attention. Some of my students murmur, "Detach, detach, detach." Or they might say, "You're getting yourself all upset. Stop what you are thinking and take time out." It's probably best to say these magic words to yourself silently, but if you need to say them out loud, do it!

The remedy your parents used during your childhood serves the very same purpose: "Hold your breath and count to ten." Some schools have a "time-out room" where disruptive students go to calm down. Go to your own time-out room. In your imagination, take a helicopter trip out of the situation. Or take a real trip to the bathroom. When you are detached from it, you can see the situation with greater perspective. Taking a long, deep breath can be the signal to yourself to pause. Pinch yourself. Set up a private signal to yourself: rub your hip, unbutton your collar, loosen your tie. Even kicking yourself can do the job. Do whatever works for you. Remind yourself in any way you can to remove yourself mentally from your present situation, stop action, and calm down. Whenever you are functioning off target, pause for as long as necessary to do some genuine problem solving.

USP Ralph Larkin uses pausing to help him tolerate the many abrasive (and unnecessary) memos from his boss. In Ralph's company, memo writing is a long-standing ritual and he is required to respond in writing to every one. But Ralph has taught himself to pause, to break his normal response pattern of getting upset.

> Whenever I receive one of those foolish memos from my boss, I say to myself, "Wait a minute, Ralph, you weren't put on this planet to get all upset. After all, you have a commitment to enjoy what you have left of your life to the hilt." I take a deep breath and I calm down, and pause to rethink. It seems that my idiot boss's memo writing is part and parcel of that short life that I'm determined to enjoy. What can I do about it? Well, I make it my business to stop

whenever I get one of those blasted things and I've learned to laugh like hell to myself. I see it as funny. Stupid. Time wasting. But funny. I've come to realize that enjoying life takes some doing, especially around here.

During the pause, Ralph reminds himself that no one need know what he's thinking. That's his private business. Ralph has learned how to keep a straight face and laugh to himself while pausing. He breaks his suffering mindset and chooses worthwhile thoughts to keep him from getting upset with a situation that is largely out of his control.

Like Ralph, most USPs have developed the fine art of tuning in things that make sense and tuning out things that don't. To non-USPs, upsetting things like foolish memos are draining, they divert much-needed energies from more useful tasks.

How Long a Pause?

How long you pause depends on how much work you have to do. If you have plenty of experience in handling the problem situation you face, you may need to pause for only a few minutes. Some problems will require you to pause for quite a long time, perhaps even months if the issue is complex. You may need only a moment's pause to break your nervousness as you step up to the podium to give that important speech. But if your career isn't working out, or your mate is leaving you, you need plenty of time to rethink about your life, maybe months.

Your pause can be in the form of a week's vacation, a sabbatical leave, a mind journey of a few minutes, or a thought that passes by in a flash. It depends on how difficult it is for you to identify the defective thoughts that caused the problem in the first place and find effective thoughts that work better. The length of the pause will depend to a large degree on your previous experience with the situation and your speed at effective thinking.

The Rest of Your Life Doesn't Stop

While you are pausing to work on one problem area, other aspects of your life do not come to a halt. You must learn to compartmentalize. While you are doing your effective-thinking detective work, the rest of your life goes on. There's work to be done, bills to be paid, meetings to attend, children to watch over. You can still keep typing, repairing, building, walking, or even talking, while you are pausing over the one issue that is giving you trouble.

USP Graham Thompson, a computer sales representative, loses out on a big sale that he had worked hard for and had expected to get. Of course he is disappointed. But he isn't paralyzed. He still continues to make sales calls, while part of him pauses to think about what he might have done differently with that one customer.

USP Paula McClennan is good at her job and she enjoys it. But her personal life is in turmoil, because her long-term relationship with her boyfriend has just ended. Paula has no difficulty taking notice (step 1) that she is not enjoying three-dimensional success, and she knows that it is time to pause, and put an end to her suffering, if she is to continue toward her goal of success. Her pause is in terms of her personal life only; she continues to work diligently and energetically at her job. During her pause (a matter of several months), Paula grieves for her loss. But because she is a USP, Paula knows that nothing will keep her from getting back on her lifetime track.

Why It Is Necessary to Pause

The main reason for pausing is to break out of your usual way of responding. It's conditioning. It's habit. And habits are very powerful things. If as you are reading this, you're in a position to cross your legs, please do so, in your customary fashion. Now, uncross your legs. Now cross them again, but this time place the opposite leg on top of the other. Probably feels a bit strange. After all, you've been crossing your legs the same way for many years.

Sometimes, when I am explaining the idea of pausing in seminars, I ask, "How many of you are familiar with Ivan Pavlov's concept of the conditioned response?" Invariably, many people raise their hands. Then I ask, "Who asked you to raise your hand?" Most of the people who raised their hands smile sheepishly. Raising hands is something we learned as little children in school; it's a matter of habit. In this situation it's like a kind of mass hypnosis.

We have all been "hypnotized" since early childhood. Our minds have been "programmed" with a wide variety of thoughts, placed there by parents, relatives, friends, teachers. If what is lurking in your subconscious mindset is working in your behalf, it makes sense not to tamper with it. But if your "programming" is working against your best interests, then it makes sense to break that mindset. Once a particular thought takes up residence in your brain, you have the right to decide whether or not to use it in your program. You can tell any thought exactly how to behave as long as it is your "property."

And that's what pausing is all about. During the pause, you rethink your habitual response. Pausing is essential if you are to break a self-limiting or self-defeating mindset. To demonstrate this, I later on ask the same audience the same question: "How many of you are familiar with Ivan Pavlov's concept of the conditioned response?" This time no hands go up. Why? Because people have had a chance to become *aware* of the conditioned response, and have decided to break the conditioning.

During the pause you remind yourself that you can consciously *choose* any thought about a stimulus that you want to. You might not be able to change the external issue, but you can always, by pausing and choosing, *think about that issue any way that you want.* When you do that, you have taken a major step toward reducing any external problem down to manageable size.

Practice Breaking Your Mindset

To better appreciate how easy it is to be victimized, even when warned, by a self-defeating mindset, try the following exercises. During your short pause, try to see if there is an alternate way of looking at the exercise that will lead to an easy solution. USPs always reserve the right to look at any situation any way they want to. I call this the capacity to have "optional illusions."

Warning: Each of the following exercises deliberately tries to mislead you. So start by pausing. Then, during that pause, try some unconventional (yet effective) thinking.

1. Without lifting your pencil off the paper try to connect the following nine dots with only four straight lines. Hint: Try a new perspective. Your mindset is probably suggesting that you stay inside the boundaries.

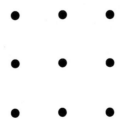

2. Answer these questions as rapidly as possible.

In order to wipe water up from the floor, one might use a _____ .
[The answer, of course, is mop.]

What does a rabbit do when it moves? *Answer:* _____.
[The answer is, hop.]

What is another name for a policeofficer that begins with a c? *Answer:* _____ . *[The answer is cop.]*

What is the first thing you do when you come to a green light? *Answer:* _____ . *[Be sure to pause before giving your answer.]*

3. How could you construct the following out of two separate blocks of wood so that they could be put together after they were manufactured separately?

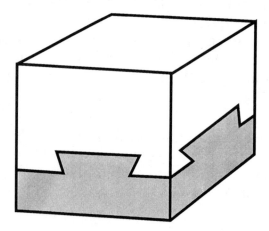

4. How do you pronounce the capital of Kentucky? Is it Louey-ville or Louis-ville?

Answers

1. To connect the nine dots in four lines, start *beyond* the normal boundary.

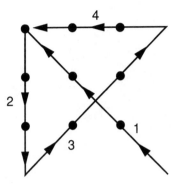

2. The answer for the last question is, of course, "go." If you did not pause, you may have found yourself quickly saying "stop."

3. The blocks can be joined if they are put together on the diagonal.

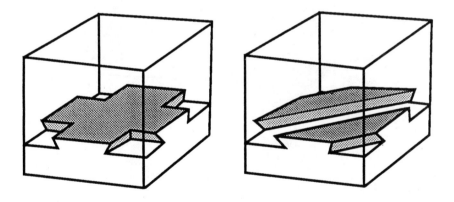

Defective	Effective
(Can't be put together)	(Slides together diagonally)

4. The capital of Kentucky is Frankfort, not Louisville.

Chapter 5

Effective Thinking, Step 3: Identify Effective Thoughts

[Shows how to identify effective thoughts that will put you back on track, toward uncommon success. Explains the subtle but important difference between effective and defective thoughts. Explains what makes a thought effective. Lists a wide range of situations, and suggests effective thoughts for each. Explains how to "string together" a combination of thoughts.]

USPs quickly turn their problems into manageable projects. The steps in a USP project are standard. First, clearly define the problem. Then, figure out a few potential solutions to that problem. Try one. If it doesn't work, try another. USP solutions always take the form of effective thoughts leading to effective action. The task now, in step 3, is to identify these effective thoughts.

Start With Self-Responsibility

USPs have a special way of gradually shifting the responsibility from the external event to themselves. For example, supposing someone is experiencing a great deal of pressure

The ET Process for Uncommon Success

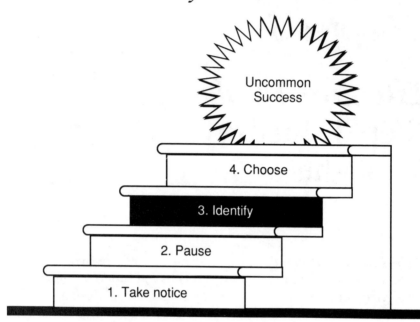

Step 3: Identify Effective Thoughts

on the job. A conventional, non-USP thinker might think, "Pressures on my job make me nervous." But in an identical situation, a USP would think, "Pressures on my job do not make me nervous. It is my *thoughts* about the pressures on my job that are making me nervous. All I need do is to identify some calming thoughts instead of tension-producing thoughts, and I won't be nervous."

Taking this kind of self-responsibility usually occurs in four stages.

Stage 1 Thinking: "Pressures on my job make me nervous." (It's doing it to me.)

Stage 2 Thinking: "I make myself nervous from the pressures on my job." (I'm doing it to me.)

Stage 3 Thinking: "More specifically, I make myself nervous from the thoughts that I and I alone choose about the pressure on my job." (The thoughts that I choose about the situation are doing it to me.)

Stage 4 Thinking: I will identify and choose calming thoughts about the pressures on my job instead of tension-producing ones."

What Makes a Thought Effective?

The bulk of this chapter is devoted to sharing an encyclopedia of effective thoughts that you can use as a base for building your own portfolio. But first it's important to review some key concepts about effective thoughts.

• *An effective thought is one that gets the intended results.* In context of the effective thinking system, a thought can be effective only if it leads you, directly or indirectly, toward uncommon success. Whether or not a particular thought does that for you depends on two factors: the external circumstances you are facing at the moment, and whether that particular thought appeals to your disposition at the time. Obviously the thought that may work well for a friend may not work in exactly the same way for you.

For example, two people have the same bad-tempered boss. One deals with him by thinking, "His bad temper is ruining his health; poor man, he's going to end up in an early grave. I'm fortunate I don't have to react to his quick temper with bad temper of my own." Another person might not find that thought effective. Instead, this other person might think, "Boy, doesn't he look silly yelling like that? If he only knew how funny he looks with his face all red and puffy." The two thoughts are very different, but they have the same result: The boss's bad temper doesn't affect the employees' well-being.

A Sampler of Directly Effective Thoughts

- When you need to calm down, to relax:
  Thought: I'm on [a golf course/a high mountain meadow/a sailboat at sunset].
- To help you tolerate the long hours spent commuting to work:
  Thought: I enjoy doing some great thinking on the way, to and from work each day.
- To help you pay more attention:
  Thought: I really need to understand what this person is saying.
- To help you stay on your diet:
  Thought: I don't like desserts now. They make me nauseous.
- To get rid of negative feelings about someone:

> *Thought:*   Take that and *that* (while punching a pillow).
> *Thought:*   I'm throwing darts at So-and-so on my imaginary dartboard.

- To boost self-confidence before a speech:
  > *Thought:*   I can already hear the applause. I'll be terrific.
- To give yourself motivation, to get your adrenalin going:
  > *Thought:*   The enemy is right on my heels; I've got to get going!
- To give yourself credit, when someone says you didn't really deserve something—that you were "just lucky":
  > *Thought:*   Luck counts!

- *Timing is important.* A particular thought can be effective because it happens to be given at just the right time. A thought that might prove effective for you in one instance might not be effective at another time or place. If you choose a thought that doesn't work as you had expected, then you must go back to your thought files and find one that does. If you don't have a thought handy, then it is your job to make one up.

- *Effective thoughts are not always positive.* Some of the difficult situation that life hands us can accurately be described as a loss: you get laid off, a parent dies, your car is stolen, you are taken off a major account at work. It is not realistic to reach for a *positive* thought in those situations, but it is very possible to choose *effective* thoughts.

We are really talking about the process of grieving. Thanks largely to the work of Dr. Elizabeth Kubler-Ross, we know that the grief process has five predictable stages: denial, bargaining, anger, depression, and then acceptance.

Denial, as a first reaction, is very normal. But the loss can't be denied. Bargaining—trying to make up for the loss—doesn't always work. You can't bargain away a broken leg, or getting fired, or someone's death. And if you can't, you *must* go through the next stages. Don't try to skip them; it will backfire later. Allow yourself to be angry, permit yourself to be depressed: these are very healthy emotions. Just make sure you don't spend more time there than is appropriate for the situation.

USPs work through the grieving process very rapidly. When they notice a loss, they quickly move past denial into bargaining. And when that proves futile, they actually force themselves to choose anger-producing thoughts. When the anger has been fully experienced, they just as quickly force themselves to choose thoughts about the loss that depress them. But they don't believe in suffering too long, so, they quickly move to acceptance.

This doesn't mean that you should put on a smiling face when you experience a loss. USPs, allow all the pain in, suffer intensely, but only for a very short time, and then they move on with their lives.

Let's look at an example. Suppose you came home from work and discovered that your house had been burglarized. Some of your treasured possessions are gone, and the place is a mess. What are your thoughts?

- "I'm ruined. I'm destroyed." Making the situation a catastrophe when it isn't, is not usually very helpful. After all, no one was killed.
- "This doesn't really bother me very much. Whoever took this stuff probably needed more than I did." This thought is not useful; it will keep you stuck in denial instead of letting you work through your very real loss.
- "I'm going to get me a gun and shoot that SOB when I find him." That will get you arrested—not very effective.
- "Let's hope this never happens again." This is not very effective either; it leaves you vulnerable for another robbery.

A USP, on the other hand, might think: This makes me furious and angry and I have a right to be furious and angry, but not for too long." Then she might move on to "I'll do everything possible to catch the culprits and take necessary precautions to see that this doesn't happen again."

• *Even "nonfactual" thoughts can be effective.* By that I mean thoughts that you know are not supported by the evidence but consciously choose because they work for you. I sometimes call them creative self-deception—using illusions in a constructive way. Since we know that what you think creates your feelings, it is sometimes useful to deceive yourself—if no one gets hurt in the process. It can help in a dentist's chair, at a boring business meeting, or at the speaker's podium. For example, if you were in prison, it might be very useful to convince yourself that you are not in a prison but on a golf course. (In fact, there is a reported case of someone actually improving his real golf game while imprisoned, by using his imagination!)

For another example of nonfactual but effective thoughts, let's go to the ballpark. "Fireball" Ennis, the best relief pitcher the Washington Avengers ever had, is warming up in the bullpen. It's the ninth inning, the bases are loaded with two outs, and the manager signals for Fireball to take the mound.

On his way out to the mound. Fireball hears the loud roar of the crowd and feels the knot in his stomach pull even tighter. And he starts talking to himself. "The hell with you, sports fans," he says softly. "I don't give a damn about this game. This is nothing but a stupid game. A game for children, not for full-grown adults. The hell with it. I hate this damed game. I hate baseball."

Filled with the fire of anger, Fireball hurls his first pitch—a fastball over the corner.

Strike one!" the umpire bellows.

"The hell with everybody," Fireball mumbles to himself.

The next pitch is a slow curve. The hitter dribbles a grounder to the second baseman for an easy out.

Fireball Ennis has saved another game. The fans go wild. Fireball touches his hat in acknowledgment of their cheers. "I love baseball," he says to himself. "I love these fans. I really love this game."

An Encyclopedia of Effective Thinking

Here, in alphabetical order, are some common life situations that could be improved through effective thinking. I borrowed these concepts and thoughts from many USPs. I hope they serve as the basis for developing your own file of effective thoughts. I have included a brief discussion of the rationale behind each concept, and suggestions on situations where you might apply them.

ANGER. Remember, fear is always the root cause of any anger that you experience. Eliminate the fear and you'll eliminate the anger. When you are too angry, try to figure out what you are afraid of. And if you find that the fear is unnecessary (as it often is) you will feel your anger evaporate almost immediately. This knowledge will also help you deal more effectively with other people when they are angry. When you encounter an angry person, don't think, "What a tough person!" Instead ask yourself, "What is he or she afraid of?"

CARING ABOUT YOURSELF. Remember, most people don't care about you nearly as much as you can care about yourself.

You'd probably worry a whole lot less about what people think of you if you only knew how rarely they do it. Other people are usually just as busy as you are, focusing mostly on themselves and their own pressing issues. This thought can help you relax under pressure and remind yourself that the whole world is not watching you.

CLOSENESS TO OTHERS. You can get close to others, but at bottom, you are fundamentally alone. Accepting this reality protects you from too much disappointment when you have counted on others a bit too much. This doesn't mean that you can't get very, very close to other people; it just means that there is a very important portion of yourself that is for you alone. Learning to live alone—together with others—is essential if you are to be uncommonly successful.

CHANGE AND ACCEPTANCE. Remember, with effective thinking you have the knowhow to change those things that can be changed and to accept those things over which you have no control. USPs take a two-pronged attack on difficulties: effective action combined with effective attitude. This thought can give you the confidence to face any adversity.

CHANGING THE WORLD. Change this world into a better place; do it by changing yourself. Idealists want to make this world a better place, and so do realistic USPs. If you want to change the world, you can. Change yourself and you will have changed the world a little bit. This thought will help you to more fully embrace the USP concept of taking total self-responsibility. It will help you do something realistic and definitely within your power about life on this planet of ours.

CYNICISM. Aim to be a healthy skeptic, not a self-sabotaging cynic.

This thought will keep you from going too far when you get discouraged. It will remind you to separate out the good before discarding the bad.

DEPRESSION. Accept some degree of depression in your

life, maybe even bring it on deliberately. But don't "hang out" there for any length of time. When experiencing a loss of any kind, you *must* go through all five stages. One of the most difficult of these stages is depression. But depression is useful. It expedites the process of working through your loss, and it awakens your consciousness about worldwide injustices and gives you incentive to do something about them if you want to.

DRAMA OF LIFE. Think of yourself as participating in the drama of life, not just the theater of life. Theater, as entertaining as it may be, is artificial. But drama is real. This thought encourages you to participate actively in life rather than stand on the sidelines as a spectator. It reminds you to take chances, to be an activist.

FACTS. You cannot ever change absolute facts. But many "facts" are relative.

This thought helps you remember that life is relative, and so consequently you can always find a perspective that fits you.

FAILURE. You never have real failures, only learning opportunities. It is those times when you fail in one of your projects that you discover your limits. And when you turn a so-called failure into learning opportunities, you will overcome all fear of failure. If you have never "failed," you are probably operating at far less than your capacity. Remind yourself, "what failed is not me, but simply one of my projects." This thought will help you make the most of setbacks and reduce the fear of failing so that you can take risks when necessary.

FAIRNESS. Remember, the world, as it is presently constructed, is not a very fair place. Do everything possible to correct unfairness when you can; when you can't, do some rapid grieving, either for yourself or others, and then get on with things. (Don't let unfairness spoil the flow of your life.)

THE FUTURE. Remind yourself periodically, "The best is yet to come." It is wise to make the most out of each present moment that you have. But if that seems difficult because things are going poorly, then look for a better future. Hope for the future can make any present moment better. It also tends to become a self-fulfilling prophecy.

GAMESMANSHIP. In business, it is better for you to be a bit of gamesman instead of a jungle fighter. Sometimes you need to lose battles in order to win wars. Sometimes a straight line is not the shortest distance between two points. By intelligent planning, organizing, and taking time to work with and through others, you can often achieve better results. This thought can help you curb any tendency to jump wildly and unthinkingly into a fray.

GUILT. Remember, guilt before the fact has value. Guilt after the fact has no value unless you can make reparations. This "guilt-in-advance" can stop you from doing something wrong. Effective thinking about guilt will also help you forgive yourself for mistakes, and keep you from repeating them.

HORIZONS. Think of aiming for a horizon instead of a boundary. The horizon continuously changes as you move toward it. You can never really ever expect to reach it, and thus you can keep going until your last day on earth. The view of the horizon is always from a distance. Boundaries are much more limiting. Use this thought to keep yourself open to seeking and learning.

HUMOR. Remember, life is much too serious to not have a sense of humor about it. Your short life is the single most important thing you will ever have, so why not enjoy the process? You can lubricate the tough times in life by laughing, especially at yourself.

HURTING. Remember, allowing yourself to occasionally become hurt and vulnerable is the price of admission into the family of humankind. This thought reminds you to care more and be more sensitive for others. Getting hurt occasionally will keep you in touch with your fellow human beings.

IDENTITY. You have a hidden inner identity (see Chapter 2) that goes beyond your job title or even your family role. Your inner identity will continue to serve you through thick and thin. It will keep you from becoming unduly upset during family strife. It will insulate you from fear of losing your job.

JEALOUSY. Remember, all jealousy is based on fear—the fear that you won't get your fair share of whatever it is that you are jealous about. If you remind yourself that you are special and unique, your jealousy will rapidly disappear. Also, reminding yourself that you are a USP and that the person you are jealous of probably is not can be most effective.

LIFE AS A JOURNEY. Remind yourself that life is best lived as a continuing journey, a process rather than an end. Your journey through life is to be enjoyed, day by day, as much as humanly possible. Take time to smell the flowers. Be sure to enjoy a portion of each day, regardless of how difficult that may sometimes seem.

LIFE PURPOSE. Remind yourself that the main purpose of your life is to realize uncommon success, that is, to enjoy your life and accomplish a few things. And to do this, if at all possible, not at the expense of any other person. USPs enjoy contributing to the quality of life on this planet.

MORE. You are a cornucopia, a veritable fountain, of ideas and opportunities. This thought will help you be more generous and feel more prolific and prosperous. You will actually believe that "there really is more where that came from," and this will help you share more freely with others. You will be less fearful that you will be used or used up.

NOW. Remember, nows are all you have ever had or ever will have. Your past is nows used up; your future is nows yet to come. All that you can really be sure of is this present moment. Your past is already subject to "selective retention," and the future is uncertain. This will help you to stop worrying excessively about your future or having useless guilt about the past.

OWNERSHIP. You don't really own anything until you can comfortably give it away. This thought will permit you to become more generous, if that is what you want to be. If you spend too much of your limited time trying to retain a possession, tangible or otherwise, making sure that no one takes it away, soon that possession begins to own you. When you give something away, you will be free to move forward to another activity, where you will do just as well—or even better. You will find this thought especially useful for sharing ideas, staying loose, being spontaneous, and going through life without feeling burdened.

THE PAST. Take the flames from the past and forget the ashes. Take the useful parts of the past, the good lessons, and discard the rest.

PREFERENCES. Prefer whatever you wish, but *need* only a very few things. The most difficult time in the world to get something is when you really need it. So it is useful to convince yourself that you need very little. Couch your deepest desires as something that you prefer, not something you need. You "need" a modicum of food, shelter, and clothing just to stay alive. But you "prefer" a reasonable quantity of very good food, a nice wardrobe, and a comfortable home. Paradoxically, when you decide you don't really need something, it's easier to get. When you take the pressure off yourself, you perform better.

PRIORITIES. Remember to edit your life regularly. You can't include everything. You can't do everything equally well, even if you wanted to. This thought can remind you to focus on quality rather than quantity. It can also help you to organize your schedule, limit your commitments, and concentrate on genuine, rather than superficial, relationships and activities. Edit your life, the same way that you might edit a paper that you have written, and you can keep from becoming overwhelmed by duties and tasks.

RATIONALIZATIONS. It's okay to have healthy rationalizations, but not unhealthy ones. You need healthy defense mechanisms to cope with the difficult aspects of this world. In fact the whole effective thinking process is essentially one big healthy defense system. Recognize that you can choose any thought whatsoever, even irrational ones, if it makes sense to do so.

REALISTIC EXPECTATIONS. You will be better off if you are realistic, and not merely reasonable. Being "reasonable" in this rather irrational world of ours can produce a very large measure of frustration. It is much wiser to be realistic. Being realistic requires you to make relatively accurate predictions about what is likely to happen. Being realistic, especially when dealing with people, means making allowance for human foibles and mistakes. Have realistic expectations about your work and about your family life, and you will not be disappointed.

RELATIONSHIPS. All your relationships with other persons are conditional: Value given for value received. This thought will serve to remind you that you can't possibly be all things to all people. That is very important, especially if you have been a "people pleaser." Clarify your own set of relationships by setting a hierarchy of value: (1) some larger force, (2) self, (3) spouse, (4) children, (5) close friends and colleagues, (6) other friends and acquaintances. Develop your own. For example, your work relationships might be: (1) your customers, (2) the "big" boss, (3) your immediate boss, (4) your staff, (5) colleagues. Don't try to pretend that you can always "be there" for everybody on an equal basis.

REJECTION. You cannot possibly be rejected by someone who doesn't listen and care for you on your own terms. If people don't really listen to you on your own terms, they don't really know you. And if they don't really know you, they cannot really reject you. They can only reject their limited perception of you—and that is *their* problem. This thought can help you stay loose when you have to give a big speech or make a business presentation. It also helps you to risk rejection in your personal life.

REPUTATION. Remember, you are not your reputation. You are not entirely in charge of what others think of you. You may be able to influence their opinion of you, but you cannot direct what they choose to think of you. You are most certainly a lot more than your mere image. You are really your hidden identity. This thought may help you minimize undue concern about what others think of you and help you worry less about gossip.

SATISFACTION. You will be infinitely better off and have a much higher quality of life if you pursue satisfaction rather than happiness. Many people go to bed hungry every night; how can we be "happy" in the face of that? It can be highly satisfying to make a condolence call on a friend who has lost a loved one, but it is certainly not a happy experience. Happiness is much easier to achieve when you do not aggressively pursue it.

STRESS. Be a eu-stress seeker and not a distress avoider. This thought is borrowed directly from Dr. Hans Selye, the Canadian stress specialist. The term *eu-stress* is derived from the Greek and means "good stress." Good stress is stimulating; it can help you move forward in your career and in your life. Distress is toxic. This thought can help you move into action, instead of either standing on the sidelines or overreacting to the tension of the situation.

SUFFERING. Suffering is optional. Suffering is strictly a result of thought choice, not the external event itself. Use this concept to remind yourself to suffer sometimes—but not too much—when things get difficult. This will help you take charge of your own reactions.

TAKING CHARGE. You are in charge of this world only from the neck up. This is the basic premise of effective thinking—you must take self-responsibility for what is going on in your own mind. It will also keep you from trying to manage the minds of others. Taking care of your own mind is a big enough job.

TREATMENT BY OTHERS. In the long run people will tend to treat you the way you teach them to treat you. Remind yourself that you don't have to always accept other people's behavior, especially their behavior toward you. You may have to take some "educational" steps. This can help you deal with bosses, colleagues, friends, family, children, doctors, clerks, and all others who have a connection with your life. *You* are in charge of how others act toward you over the long haul.

UNIQUENESS. Remind yourself that you are special and unique. This will help you hold onto your self-esteem, even when things get difficult. It will also help you to overcome jealousy. "I may not have that, but at least I'm me—special and unique."

VALUES. Remember, a value is better caught than taught. Let this thought inspire you to set an example for others whom you want to influence. Instead of trying to lecture them, show your values by the way you behave. This will keep you from becoming too "preachy" or expecting too much just because you gave lip service to something.

VICTIM. Stubbornly refuse to let yourself feel like a victim. This is a major principle of USPs. You are in charge of your life. Be sure to trick yourself back into the driver's seat—even when you really have been temporarily "victimized." Remember that you can choose thoughts and figure out a way of handling any circumstance (good or bad) that life dishes up. *You* are in control—not others, not outside circumstances, not fate.

WORK AND PLAY. Remind yourself to work hard but play harder. There's nothing wrong with working hard, but remind yourself now and then that there is more to life than just work. Your main purpose is to live a life that is uncommonly successful: *some* work and *plenty* of life satisfaction.

WORRY. Always replace excessive worry with due concern. Due concern can help you to be more sensitive and caring. It will help you to prepare in advance, and keep you on your toes. Worry "a little," when it helps, but stop worrying when it is useless, simply by replacing worry with due concern.

Create a Line of Effective Thoughts

I don't have to tell you that much of what we deal with in this life of ours is quite complex. Sometimes just one effective thought is not enough. For tough situations, you may need to develop a line, or battery, by stringing together a series of related thoughts. No matter how difficult things seem, there is a combination of effective thoughts that will work.

Take, as an example, this job-related issue: You feel underappreciated by your boss. Give yourself these thoughts:

> The most difficult time to get something, it seems to me, is when I really need it. When was it hardest to get a job? When I really needed one. And the same holds for having my boss appreciate me. It is hardest for me to have her appreciate my good work when I really need her to do that. So, my philosophy from this point on is that I don't really need her to appreciate my good work. I just prefer that she did.

> And in order to get over the fact that she doesn't really appreciate my good work, I'm going to grieve just as rapidly as possible. I'm beyond denial and bargaining. I'll make myself get deliberately angry and then I'll force myself into depression for a few days. Then I'll get on with it and continue to enjoy my work life.

> After all, I'm not entirely responsible for the way that Ms. Barkly perceives me. She's in charge of her own view of the world and of me. And I'm in charge of my own view. I am fiercely determined to make my life work. I have a commitment to a life of uncommon success, even in the face of lack of appreciation.

> Besides, it really isn't me that is not being appreci-

ated. It's my boss's image of me that is not what I would like it to be. And I'm not entirely in charge of my image. If she really knew me, I mean really knew me and the quality of work that I do, she would have to appreciate me. But she just doesn't know. At least at this point. Which reminds me. There are probably a few things I can do to call my good work to her attention.

So, this person uses a line of effective thoughts to move into effective action.

Another circumstance that may require a string of effective thoughts is the breakdown of a long-term relationship. First, let's look at some defective thoughts that are likely to occur. Then we'll identify effective thoughts to counteract them:

"I can't believe she doesn't really care for me as much as I thought. I'm crushed. I thought we were really connected, that we had something special, that we were one. But I was wrong. I feel awful. I'm a failure at love. It's all over. I hurt terribly. I'm nothing without her. Life has no meaning."

Now consider this counter string of effective thoughts:

"This relationship wasn't a failure, it was a worthwhile, although hard to take, learning experience. In spite of it, I think that the best is yet to come. My future is unlimited. Staying with her was a confinement. In a strange way, all this is funny. Life is much too short not to have a sense of humor about it. And, I have an identity that goes far beyond this relationship. I know who I am, and it doesn't depend one iota on my relationship with her."

Doesn't it become clear how this string of effective thoughts can empower a person? Even when trying to deal with the inevitability of one's death, you will find that effective thinking provides a new source of energy to help you make the most of your life—whether you are a twenty-eight-year-old contemplating the next forty to fifty years, or a person entering late middle-age who sees death as an eventuality that will be coming sooner, rather than later. All USPs understand that it makes no sense to spend their relatively "short vacation from eternity" worrying about it. And so they do everything they can to make their lives happy and successful.

You have now completed the first three steps of the ET process. Only one more step left to go: actually choosing the thoughts that you have identified. In the next chapter, I will show you how to do just that.

Chapter 6

Effective Thinking, Step 4: Choose

[Shows how to actively choose (either consciously or subconsciously), the effective thoughts that were identified in the previous step. To explain how thought choosing works, the Body-Mind Theater is explained. Teaches three methods for thought choosing: free will, reverse psychology, and self-hypnosis to access the subconscious.]

Choosing a particular thought is a privilege available only to human beings. All other animals are limited to their innate conditioning and instinct. But you and I can transcend our conditioning and choose any thought we want to, any time, any place. Yet, sadly, only a very small percentage of humans have learned to take full advantage of this special power.

You Are Responsible for Your Thoughts

The human mind is a remarkable instrument. It has been estimated that we have some 10 billion neurons in our brain, each theoretically capable of housing one thought (either effective, defective, or neutral). The vast majority of those thoughts are housed in our subconscious. In 1959, Dr. W. Penfield, a neurosurgeon, discovered that our brains have recorded, much like a tape recorder, every perception we

The ET Process for Uncommon Success

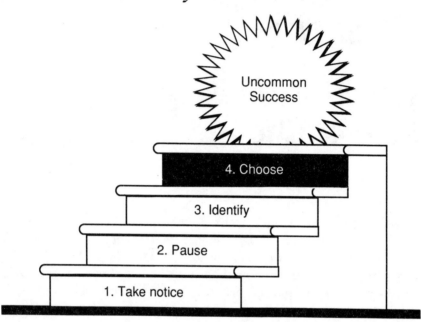

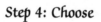

Step 4: Choose

ever had. Somewhere in your subconscious is a record of what your mother was cooking, and what it smelled like, the first time you crawled into the kitchen.

The subconscious is very powerful indeed. For many years, it has recorded messages from parents, teachers, friends. These programmed thoughts can be encouraging, confidence building, and supportive, or they can be defective and self-defeating. For example, there are many attractive people walking around who think they are ugly, because of some message they got when they were very young; and nothing can convince them otherwise.

When those defective subconscious thoughts get in the way of your good life, you need to reprogram them. That is not easy, of course, but it can be done. You can actually teach your subconscious mind to ignore its defective thoughts and fill it instead with effective thoughts.

The first step is to accept the fact that you are responsible for all your thoughts, even the subconscious ones. USPs always take full responsibility for what is in their head, even for the involuntary thoughts that seem to rise up spontaneously out of their subconscious. Technically they did not consciously choose those thoughts, but they allowed them a forum, and that's what counts.

Whenever a defective thought comes to your mind, it is up to you to decide whether to permit it to stay. After all, whose head is it? If you entertain a defective thought (no matter where it came from), you are responsible for the defective feelings and defective behavior that will inevitably follow.

Can People Choose Their Thoughts?

If you still have some lingering doubt that it is actually possible to choose what thoughts are in your mind, relax—that's normal. You *can* choose your thoughts, and I will demonstrate this to you if you will try one simple experiment. Remember that we live our lives one minute at a time. This is going to be a one-minute experiment.

Instead of permitting the next minute of your life to be just ordinary, insist on making it extraordinary. The key, of course, to making this next minute very rich and very satisfying lies entirely within you. It depends entirely on the thoughts that you choose. To do the experiment, stop now and line up some wonderful thoughts. Maybe you see a child's face, smiling at you. How about a thought about having a great success? Getting that long-sought contract, making the sale, or getting that promotion? How about some thoughts about the beauty of nature? One of your favorite sunsets or views from the mountains on that ski slope? Whatever gives you pleasure.

Now, assuming you've lined up a few joyful thoughts, take the next minute to actually choose some of them. Shut your eyes so that your imagination has free reign and then begin. Make this next minute a very pleasing minute in your life. Okay, begin. Take a minute out to give yourself some genuine pleasure by thinking one of the thoughts you lined up.

Now, let's rate your level of satisfaction for this one-minute experience that you just gave yourself. (1 is low and 10 is high). The higher the better, of course. If your score for this minute was 6 or better, congratulations—you did better than average. If you can improve the quality of your life by thought choosing for one minute, then why not for an hour, a year, a lifetime?

Three Choosing Methods

Assuming you're now convinced it is possible to choose your thoughts, exactly how do you go about it? There are three techniques for choosing thoughts:

1. Conscious choice. By your own free will, or will-power, you consciously, willfully choose the effective thought or thoughts that you had prepared in step 3.

2. Reverse psychology. Tell yourself to think the *opposite* of what you really want to think. (Try, for the next ten seconds, *not* to think of a red elephant.)

3. Self-hyponosis, to give you direct access to your own subconscious.

Let's consider each method.

Consciously Choosing

Sometimes simply identifying effective thoughts (step 3) is enough; you create an effective thought, and it seems you automatically choose it. But often it is necessary to exercise willpower, and to repeat the particular thought several times before it really sinks in.

Visualization can help. We think with pictures as well as with words. Visualize yourself successfully dealing with any condition that is giving you trouble. Suppose you have a very abrasive boss and when he is nearby you become extremely nervous and make mistakes. The issue then would be overcoming your nervousness when the boss is around.

Shut your eyes and imagine your boss peering over your shoulder while you are trying to work. When you can actually feel yourself getting nervous, signal that fact to yourself by extending your forefinger. This will take a moment or two. Then open your eyes and relax your hands and rest a bit.

Then shut your eyes again, but this time imagine your boss peering over your shoulder *without* you getting nervous. This will probably take a bit longer, but when you can successfully picture this happening, open your eyes.

Then reflect on what you were thinking the second times. Were you ignoring him? Were you thinking that he was silly or unimportant? Or were you simply thinking concentrating entirely on the job in front of you? Whatever it was, those are effective thoughts you can choose whenever the event actually happens. Practice using effective visualizations for any disturbing factor. Then when an actual circumstance occurs, you will have some effective thoughts ready that you can consciously choose.

Because thought choosing is such a revolutionary idea, most people need practice to get good at it. Here's a way to motivate yourself to practice.

List a few activities that you enjoy, such as watching TV, playing a certain sport, eating a special dessert, visiting with someone special.

_____

_____

Then list a few activities that you do not enjoy, such as cleaning the house or paying bills.

_____

_____

Now, make a contract with yourself, using the activities that you like to do as rewards and the things you find onerous as punishments, and put it in writing.

I, [your name], promise to practice effective thought choosing regularly. If I do, I will receive the following rewards: _____

_____

If I do not practice, I will penalize myself as follows:

_____

_____

Reverse Psychology

If consciously choosing effective thoughts (or pictures) doesn't always work for you, try reverse psychology. This thought-choosing technique requires you to make things get worse, in order to make them eventually get better. For example, a common way to help a stutterer overcome the condition is to instruct him to exaggerate it, actually stuttering even more, and then ask him if he likes what he is doing to himself.

If you can't sleep at night, instead of trying harder to choose sleep-producing thoughts, choose thoughts that will really *wake you up*. Then you ask yourself, "Do I like what I am doing to myself?" If you do, keep choosing thoughts to keep you awake. If not, stop. Then, having taken full charge of yourself, once again consciously choose sleepy thoughts.

Self-Hypnosis

If you have not been successful with either free will or reverse psychology, your next step is to call on your subconscious. Consciously repeating an effective thought to yourself over and over again doesn't always work. And the reason for that is quite uncomplicated. The program in your subconscious mind is rejecting the thought that you are trying to choose and sending other thoughts up to the foreground of your conscious mind in its place. You need to reprogram your subconscious mind, and you can do it with a method of rapid self-hypnosis. It takes all of ninety seconds. I have successfully taught this self-hypnosis to many of my clients. Once you have identified an effective thought or two that you would like to inject into your subconscious, you can always use this method.

Your conscious mind is really just a thin but tough layer that covers the much larger subconscious. The way to get past the protection of your conscious (sometimes overly skeptical) mind is to temporarily confuse and baffle it, stun it, and get it out of operation, and then quickly slip your preselected effective thoughts right past it and into the sub-conscious (see Figure 6-1).

First you relax the conscious mind, then divert it using a process called creative self-deception. Then, while your con-scious mind is diverted, enter the effective thought directly into your subconscious. Finally, move back into conscious-ness, with your subconscious now safely reprogrammed.

Let's try it.

Step 1:   *Relax.* The first step in rapid self-hypnosis is to relax the conscious mind. Take a deep breath, make your forehead very tight, and then relax it. That's all you have to do; you do not have to be in a deep hypnotic trance. After you have relaxed

Figure 6-1. The self-hypnosis process.

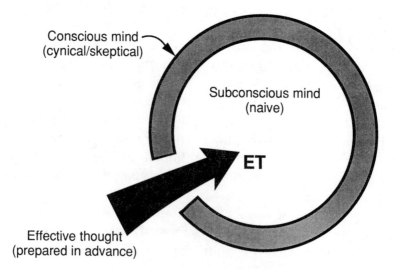

just a bit, say the word "enter" to yourself. Think of the "enter" key on the computer. You are entering that thought ("Relax") into your mental programming.

Step 2:   *I Can't Separate My Two Fingers."* Hold your thumb and forefinger together and say to yourself, "No matter how hard I try, I cannot separate my two fingers." Then try very hard to separate them but *don't do it.* This is where creative self-deception comes into play. Your skeptical, conscious mind will be telling you, "Nonsense. You can separate your fingers." Don't listen. Your aim is to confuse your conscious mind and bypass it. Then say again "Enter."

Step 3:   *Repeat the Effective Thought Three Times.* Now that you have direct access to your own subconscious, inject into it the effective thought that you prepared in advance. Repeating it to yourself three times, each time more forcefully. You can also tell any defective thoughts that you may have identified to remain quiet and take a back seat because you are just not going to use them.

Step 4:   *Wake Up.* Now you simply separate your fingers and say to yourself, "OK, I'm reprogrammed now. Enter." And, with your fingers fully functioning, do enter the real world with your subconscious effectively reprogrammed. This reprogramming can be expected to last about fourteen hours, and then you'll have to do it again, until the effective thoughts that you put in really take root. It is also possible to do this several times each day—if practical for you.

Now let's use the rapid self-hypnosis method to help you deal with a real situation. Start by writing down an issue (personal or professional) that you are facing. It can be major

issue or minor. Perhaps it involves your working environ-
ment, getting along with someone on your job, your boss, a
colleague, or a friend. Or it can be a personal issue such as
your fitness level or worry about your children.

An issue that is currently giving me some aggravation: _____

_____

_____

_____

_____

What are some effective thoughts that will help me with this
issue?

_____

_____

_____

_____

_____

_____

Step 1:   Say to yourself, "Relax."

Step 2:   Say to yourself, "I can't separate my fingers."

Step 3:   Repeat the effective thought three times, each time
saying it more strongly.

Step 4:   Say to yourself, "OK, now I can separate my fingers.
[*Do so.*] Then say to yourself, "I'm reprogrammed
now. Enter."

And that's it, for at least the next fourteen hours. You've
given yourself a new tool for choosing. You still must exercise

will power regarding that thought, but at least you've stacked the odds in your favor.

How Your Mind Works: The Body-Mind Theater

To better understand thought choosing, it might be helpful to see the process at work in a model of the mind that I call the Body-Mind Theater. The Body-Mind Theater replicates what goes on in your body and mind, and your resulting behavior.

Let's go into the theater and see who and what is involved. (Figure 6-2 is a plan of the theater.) We'll identify the cast of characters and establish some theater "house rules."

In the center of the theater stands the Program Director—that's you. As Program Director you are the "thought-chooser" for the Body-Mind Theater. It is your job to produce an excellent, uncommonly successful life program. You have absolute authority to make the final decision about what thought, waiting backstage, can come to the podium to speak to the theater audiences—your feelings (F).

The Hook is for use by you, the Program Director, as a thought-stopping and thought-choosing device. At any time you can use it to push or pull a thought to or from the Podium. The Podium, of course, stands in front of the audience. It's where the Thought-Speaker speaks. Only one thought is permitted to occupy the podium at any particular time.

Now, let's raise the curtain and see how things come into play. Waiting backstage, you can see all of your thoughts—both effective and defective (ET and DT)—vying to get to the podium. They are located in three sections: easy access, moderate access, and difficult access. All your feelings are in the audience. They too are divided into three sections: upper-body feelings, mid-body feelings, and lower body feelings. Your feelings are highly impressionable; they

Figure 6-2. The Body-Mind Theater.

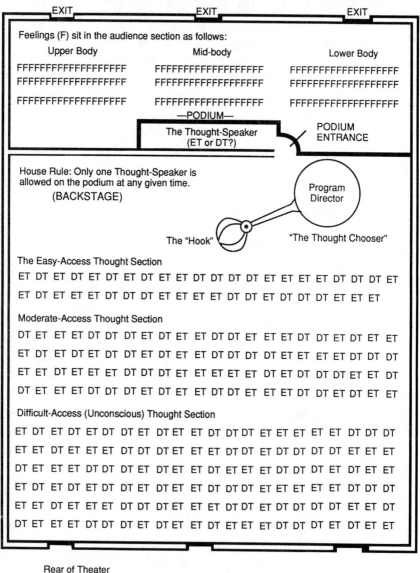

The "real" outside world—The Realm of External Behavior (B)

BBBBBBBBBBBBBBBBBBBBBBBBBBBBBBBBBBBBBBBBBBBBBBBBBBBBBBBBBBBBBB
BBBBBBBBBBBBBBBBBBBBBBBBBBBBBBBBBBBBBBBBBBBBBBBBBBBBBBBBBBBBBB
BBBBBBBBBBBBBBBBBBBBBBBBBBBBBBBBBBBBBBBBBBBBBBBBBBBBBBBBBBBBBB

EXIT   EXIT   EXIT

Feelings (F) sit in the audience section as follows:

Upper Body   Mid-body   Lower Body

FFFFFFFFFFFFFFFFFFFFF   FFFFFFFFFFFFFFFFFFFFF   FFFFFFFFFFFFFFFFFFFFF
FFFFFFFFFFFFFFFFFFFFF   FFFFFFFFFFFFFFFFFFFFF   FFFFFFFFFFFFFFFFFFFFF
FFFFFFFFFFFFFFFFFFFFF   FFFFFFFFFFFFFFFFFFFFF   FFFFFFFFFFFFFFFFFFFFF

—PODIUM—

The Thought-Speaker
(ET or DT?)

PODIUM
ENTRANCE

House Rule: Only one Thought-Speaker is
allowed on the podium at any given time.
        (BACKSTAGE)

Program
Director

The "Hook"   "The Thought Chooser"

The Easy-Access Thought Section

ET DT ET DT ET DT ET DT ET ET DT DT DT DT ET ET ET ET DT DT DT ET
ET DT ET ET ET DT DT DT ET ET ET ET DT DT ET DT DT DT ET ET ET

Moderate-Access Thought Section

DT ET ET ET DT DT DT ET DT ET ET DT DT ET ET ET DT DT ET DT ET ET
ET DT ET DT ET DT DT ET DT ET ET DT DT DT DT ET ET ET ET DT DT DT
ET ET DT ET ET ET DT DT DT ET ET ET ET ET DT ET DT DT DT DT ET ET DT
DT ET ET ET DT DT DT ET DT ET ET DT DT ET ET ET ET DT DT ET DT ET

Difficult-Access (Unconscious) Thought Section

ET DT ET DT ET DT DT ET DT ET ET DT DT DT ET ET ET ET ET DT DT DT
ET ET DT ET ET ET DT DT DT ET ET ET DT DT ET DT DT DT DT ET ET ET
DT ET ET ET DT DT DT ET DT ET ET DT ET ET ET DT DT DT ET DT ET ET
ET DT ET DT ET DT DT ET DT ET ET DT DT DT ET ET ET ET ET DT DT DT
ET ET DT ET ET ET DT DT DT ET ET ET DT DT ET DT DT DT DT ET ET DT
DT ET ET ET DT DT DT ET DT ET ET DT ET ET ET DT DT DT ET DT ET ET

Rear of Theater

always follow the instructions of the thought-speaker on the podium. Finally, beyond the stage doors, in the "real world," is your behavior (B), which occurs outside of your Body-Mind Theater.

Your main challenge is to get as many effective thoughts as possible into the easy-access section. Some defective thoughts are sure to try and bully their way toward the Podium, so, take charge. Use the Hook to yank them back. Give that effective thought a chance! Be careful—defective thoughts may try and disguise themselves as effective thoughts ("I need a relationship" rather than "I prefer a relationship."). You must listen carefully to the thought-speaker on the podium. If the speaker begins speaking defensively, act swiftly. Take out the hook, and pull!

You're going to have to go into training to become an excellent program director. You'll need courage to send out the Hook when a defective thought-speaker is filling the audience—your feelings—with destructive self-defeating nonsense. You want to become competent at managing your Body-Mind Theater because it's *your* show. And since this show will continue throughout your lifetime, you want to ensure that the thoughts on your program lead to the high quality of life that you owe yourself.

Here are eight different types of Program Directors. Which one would you like to have in charge of your program?

1. *The Chicken.* I'm afraid to run the show. I hope nice thoughts get on the podium, but I can't do anything about it if they don't.
2. *The Fool.* Let's have fun. Any thought that wants a turn, be my guest.
3. *The Quitter.* I resign. I'm just not up to this. Please do the show without me.
4. *The Fraud.* I just want it all to look good. You look like an effective thought, just from appearances alone. I'll just choose you.

5. *The Behavior-Pecked.* Those outside forces made me choose those thoughts.
6. *The Feelings-Pecked.* My feelings made me choose that thought.
7. *The Ghost.* I was never in charge and I never will be in charge. I have no idea who is in charge. Whoever said I was in charge?
8. *The Wise Czar.* I am definitely in charge and I mean business. I am determined to program a winning show. Hey, you, over there, Effective Thought—I'm putting you on the podium. Get ready to do a great job. Sorry, Mr. Defective Thought, here's the hook. OK, Effective Thought, the spotlight is on you. Do your thing.

The Wise Czar has many qualities worth emulating when it comes to running your own Body-Mind Theater. First, the Czar knows the difference between an effective and defective thought. The Czar knows when to take charge and when to rest. The Czar gives sufficient rope, but is always capable of putting out the hook on any thought that proves defective. Loyal to the purposes of the Body-Mind Theater, the Czar is determined to produce a program that provides inner calm, a clear sense of purpose, and plenty of adventure. This most effective Program Director produces a program that is about uncommon, three-dimensional success, and never at the expense of anyone else.

Chapter 7

Effective Thinking in Action: High Job Performance, Satisfaction, and Success

[Shows how you can apply the ET process to any difficult situation you face in your work life. Explains how USPs become high performers (success dimension #1) by having high, largely independent standards. Also explains how USPs manage to enjoy their work so much (success dimension #2) by using the ET process. Presents various case histories. Provides two checklists to help you pinpoint your own work-related issues.]

Putting the ET process to work in real life takes two kinds of action: internal and external. Both internal action (thinking effectively) and the external action (behaving effectively) are systemic to the ET process. The ET process provides you with a way to have an effective attitude, and an effective attitude permits you to take whatever effective external action is possible. And even if no effective external action is possible, at least internal action is.

How to Be a High Performer

High performance in the job is an integral part of uncommon success. USPs are high-performing workers, not by accident, but because they have *decided* to be.

The ET Process for Uncommon Success

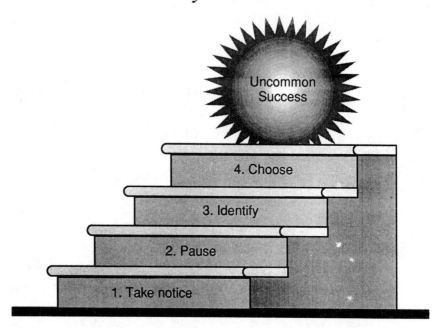

Put the Four Steps of the ET Process to Work in
Your Professional Life

USP Ken Wilkins, who has held various jobs on his way to "a better one," says, "I have found it just as easy to do high-quality work as it is to do mediocre work. But doing high-quality work is more fun. And since I'm on my job for many hours every day, I just see to it that I learn to do it very well."

USPs pursue their passion. The prefer to find work that is a perfect match with their natural aptitudes and talents. But even while they look for the perfect match, they make sure they still are high performers on the various jobs along the way. It doesn't necessarily matter what level that work is. USPs believe that if the person doing the work is dignified, then the work is dignified as well. If a USP works as a waiter while going to school, he makes sure he does an excellent job of waiting on tables.

Using the ET process, it is possible to *create* high performance. I call it "Attitude beating aptitude."

When I was in high school, there was one classmate, Billy, who was very awkward at athletics. Yet he had a dream of being an excellent basketball player—and he made it.

Looking back, I see now that Billy used the ET process to reach his goal. First he *decided* that he would be a very good basketball player. Then he took notice (step 1) that he wasn't moving toward that goal, then he paused (step 2). During his pause, he worked on the problem of how to become a very good player, while the rest of his life went on. During the pause he identified effective thoughts (step 3) and chose them (step 4). His line of effective thoughts gave him the motivation to practice shooting baskets longer and harder than any of his friends. And sure enough, after more than two years of practice, Billy made the varsity basketball team.

Now if you're less than five feet tall, you probably won't make the pros. But you can certainly play much better than you do now if you really wnat to. Or be a better speaker, or writer, or painter, or typist, or draftsman, or photographer, or salesman. It's estimated that even the best performers use only about 1 or 2 percent of their endowed talent. So if you use 20 or 30 percent of your talent, you will leave behind many others who had more natural talent to begin with. Attitude breeds aptitude. And don't forget, attitude is free.

USPs are high performers because they value high performance and set that as a goal. They have tremendous determination, and they know how to edit their lives. They study the job to be done, and then somehow manage to create a special niche for themselves, a place where they can excel. They know that life is too short to wait for the conditions to be perfect.

Nora Walters, a management consultant based in Dallas, attained her level of excellent job performance by doing an "end run."

Nora, who earned a Ph.D. degree in organizational development from the University of Southern California, set as her goal becoming a speaker for one of the country's top management consulting firms. Unfortunately, she found it difficult to break into the highly competitive "platform circuit" in management training. So, for seven years, she worked with a Texas-based management consulting firm as the director of training, and made it her business to do excellent work in the administrative role. At the same time, she kept her eye out for opportunities and offered to fill in when one of the regular speakers missed a session. Soon she became indispensable as a substitute speaker. Eventually—no great surprise—she was offered the job of trainer in the presidential and senior executive training division.

USP Al Glover was twenty-nine years old when he graduated from college, and the best job open to him at the time was brick-layer. He had a life plan built around his natural talents, but he wasn't able to find the kind of work he planned on. The bricklaying job paid well, and he had a wife and a brand-new baby to support.

I realized that I had a choice. I could take the

bricklaying job and really do it well, and then leave it when the job opportunity that I really wanted came along. Or, I could just do a fair job, and then leave when something better opened up. Or as a poor third choice, I could do it poorly, or just enough to barely get by. But for me, the only choice that made any sense was to take the job and do it very, very well. It's not that I had to perform well. It is just that I wanted to. It's my way.

Here's how Al used the ET process. He took notice (step 1) that he was not moving toward his professional goal, and that he was making himself miserable. So he paused (step 2) and broke his self-defeating mindset. In step 3 he identified a number of effective thoughts that helped him reach high performance as a bricklayer. "I find bricklaying challenging and intriguing. There's a lot to learn here. I feel strong doing physical work. This job gives me a very good chance to be alone with my thoughts and I enjoy what I think." Then he consistently chose (step 4) the thoughts that had maximum payoff for his circumstance.

USPs define excellence according to their own high standards. They realize that there are objective, external measures, but they reserve the right to be the sole judge of the quality of their own work. USPs like to believe that they have a much better and deeper understanding of their own abilities and achievements than any outsider could possibly have.

USP Joe Lawrence, a lawyer from Georgia, found a part of his work in which he knew he could excel—preparing high-quality briefs. "What the court thinks of my work is, of course, very important. If my legal briefs didn't hold up in court then I'd be out of a job, no question about that. But, I want to do better than the bare minimum. In my mind, the final determination of the excellence of my work lies within me."

How to Have a High Level of Job Satisfaction

In addition to being very high performers at whatever they happen to do for a living, USPs are determined to thoroughly enjoy their work as well. Once they take a job, they make it their business to get as much satisfaction as possible. They actually program themselves in advance to have a psychologically rich and highly satisfying day each day at work, in spite of whatever difficulties might arise.

Job satisfaction is always a matter of attitude.

USP Jennifer Barnstow works as a waitress while preparing for a career in show business, and she has consciously decided to enjoy it. She says, "If I don't enjoy what I'm doing on the path to my goal, I'll have wasted part of my life."

Even the most difficult work can prove satisfying. In all the following cases, you will find USPs using the ET process to gain satisfaction. First they take notice of when they are not enjoying their work, then they pause and identify job-satisfaction effective thoughts—and then they actively choose them.

USP Bill Cousins, a transportation supervisor, says, "This job can be pretty awful, given the impossible traffic jams we have in this city. But I still invent ways to enjoy my job. I just have to be more creative on some days than others."

USP Dawn Simon, a personnel manager, was assigned the miserable task of instituting seven-hundred job layoffs over a three-month period.

That was one of the most difficult things I've ever had to do and I hope that I never have to go through it again. Imagine, firing loyal, hard workers because of a severe market turndown that they had nothing to do with. You might say that it is impossible to that with any degree of job satisfaction. But since I have a commitment to find satisfaction in my work, I had to find a way, and I did. I made it my business to be as helpful, humane, and caring as anyone could possibly be in my position. I saw to it that they received the best outplacement benefit package possible.

USP Lenore Scott loved her work—but was starting to feel burned out.

I've been a librarian for over fifteen years. It's not only what I do for a living—it's where I spend most of my waking hours. I used to love just being around books. But after ten years with books, the flame kind of died out.

That's when I had to find something else to make my work life enjoyable. And that's when I discovered that I really liked people, even more than my books. I make it my business now to pay attention to the people who come in looking for a particular book or doing some kind of research. I decided to take a personal interest in each one of them and did all that I could do to help. I like to watch the expressions on their faces as they wrestle with ideas. I have found a whole new excitement in the people who use my services. Amazing.

Some "Hands-On" Practice in Using the ET Process

Here are some cases drawn from actual clients who came seeking help for work-related issues. Using what you have learned thus far about the ET process, try to figure out what you would do if you were in their shoes. Try to identify a few effective thoughts for each case. Jot your ideas down, on a piece of paper or in the space that I've provided. After that, I will share with you my own recommendations.

Case Number One: Jim

Jim Dunnage was the quality control manager for a major chemical company. He was married and had two children. While Jim was not the best of students in high school, in college he settled down and became a dean's list student. Actually, when Jim was younger, he had a bit of an inferiority complex, but with each of his accomplishments, and as the years progressed, that basic feeling of inferiority diminished more and more.

Jim had been with the same company for over ten years and he was told that he was targeted for promotion to the head of department within the year. Jim worked long hours and always gave that little bit extra. He felt that eventually his extra efforts would be rewarded. But when time came for Jim to get the promised promotion—he was bypassed. At first, he was numb. Then his numbness turned to fury and anger. Anger over all the extras that he had done for the company, and for which he had never been rewarded. Anger at his bosses. The system. The company. As a result, he became short tempered and even displayed anger at his wife and his children.

What would you do, if you were Jim? How would you use the four steps of the ET process to help yourself?

_____

_____

_____

_____

My recommendation: If you were Jim, I'd remind you to remind yourself that uncommon success is worth pursuing.

Then institute the ET Process as follows. Step 1: Notice that you are really making yourself quite upset because you are very ambitious and your advancement seems to be blocked. Pause, to break this self-defeating mindset, and remind yourself of this effective thought: "I wasn't put on this earth to suffer." Then identify thoughts about the rapid grieving method. Face it: Your present job is a big disappointment to you. Use rapid grieving to deal with the loss of your bright expectations. Speed up denial, bargaining, anger, and depression.

Now go to step four, and actively choose thoughts about the rapid grieving process. Go deliberately into the denial phase. Say to yourself, "I can't believe that I permitted myself to get caught up in this dead-end job." Then to bargaining, say to yourself a few times, "I've got to look elsewhere for opportunities, or if possible, make some kind of miracle happen here." Then force yourself into the anger phase; say to yourself, "I'm disgusted and furious with myself for not seeing ahead and predicting this." After that, enter the depression stage; say over and over again, "I feel rotten and miserable because of my entrapment." Then as soon as possible, move to acceptance. Say to yourself a number of times, "This is a reality that I have learned to accept. I may not love it, but I can deal with it. I'll take the givens and work it positive from this point on. Dead-end job or not, I'm going to make the very best of this circumstance. It's not really a trap, it's a learning opportunity."

Then, to enable you to enjoy your job each day that you are on it, do a second round. Go back to step 3 and identify other effective thoughts, perhaps:

I don't need to enjoy this job, I just prefer to enjoy it.
I'm on my short vacation from eternity, even on this job.
Be realistic about this job and career, not merely reasonable.
Work hard, but play harder.

My job title is not who I really am.

My primary goal is to have a rich and satisfying life-by choosing thoughts that produce inner calm, purpose, and adventure.

Using this line of effective thinking put Jim back into an enthusiastic mode of life. He found pockets of opportunity to once again begin to enjoy work. He focused on helping his staff in their own personal and professional development. He stopped dwelling entirely on himself and took an interest in others. He began managing the local Little League team and found it to be an excellent outlet for his management ambitions. He became a better listener—to his family members and to "his people" back at work. After a time, the fact that he didn't get his promotion lost its importance. Then one day, a year later, the unexpected happened. The president of the company came to Jim's office, closed the door and offered him the job of divisional manager, a much higher-level job than Jim aspired to. "Funny," Jim thought to himself. "It's surprising how it is that when you really need something it is very hard to come by. But, when you just prefer it, it just seems to come your way."

Case Number Two: Diane

Teaching was no longer very enjoyable for Diane Winters. Diane had been teaching for over fifteen years and she was tired: tired of the drudgery of teaching the same subject in the same school all those years, tired of the school administration, tired of the endless discipline problems, the lack of appreciation from the parents, and tired of the low pay. Her morale was at it's lowest ebb ever. She wondered how she could ever finish out the year.

Diane was married with three children. Her husband, Bob, was also under lots of pressure on his job. Sometimes Diane felt she was going to burst with all the pressures. Her fourth grade class was not easy to manage—especially this year. There was a clique of six boys in that class that were practically unmanageable.

What steps would you take if you were Diane?

_____

_____

_____

_____

My recommendation: It's time to pause and choose more effective thoughts. Since you are experiencing a very high level of stress, it's best if you tackle each situation, one at a time. The normal pressure of managing a job, a home, a husband, and three young children is enough to overwhelm anyone.

Here are some thoughts that I think have particular meaning to your case. Give some consideration to those that seem to have the most appeal to you. Then practice choosing those you find most applicable.

You have a hidden identity that goes beyond being a teacher or even your family role.

Remind yourself that your life is journey, a process, rather than an ends.

Remind yourself that the main purpose of your life is to realize uncommon success, that is, to enjoy your life and accomplish a few things. And to do this not at the expense of any other person.

Stubbornly refuse to let yourself feel like a victim.

Remember to edit your life regularly. You can't include everything.

You will be better off if you are realistic and not merely reasonable.

Suffering is optional.

In the long run people will tend to treat you the way you teach them to treat you. This includes the school administrator, as well as the students in your class.

Always replace excessive worry with due concern.

Case Number Three: Bart

Bart Livingston, the star quarterback of the Zeniths, was badly injured during the first game of the season. When the team doctor broke the bad news that the injury would keep him out for the rest of the season, he fell into a depression. Bart, known for his positive mental attitude, was in trouble. "I never felt this depressed before in my entire life. And trying to smile about it just makes me feel worse. The trouble is, depression has just never been in my vocabulary."
  What would you do, if you were in Bart's place?

_____

_____

_____

_____

My advice: Very few people can get through this world of ours without at least some depression. Some depression can actually be good for you. It can help you come to understand your loss. You can use it to make yourself a more compassionate and caring person. And you can use it to help you clarify what you want to do when football is over. This terrible incident can bring you in touch with the reality that you can't play this game all your life. Find yourself an inner identity that goes beyond the playing of football. Use rapid self-hypnosis to teach yourself, at the subconscious level, that depression is a very healthy place for you to visit once in a while.

Case Number Four: Harry

Harry Martin wasn't really all that old, but hard times had aged him prematurely. You could see the sadness in his tired eyes and in the way he walked. For the past twenty years, Harry Martin carried the entire weight of building a successful business on his not-so-broad shoulders. And now, Harry was very bitter. He had worked hard to build a reputation of excellent service, but all that was gone now, since he allowed Andy Eagen to become an equal partner. Harry had thought that Eagen's investment and ideas would help the business grow, but the exact reverse happened. In just a matter of months Eagen had destroyed Harry's reputation for integrity. And because of the legalities of the situation, there wasn't a thing Harry could do about it. The business that Harry had worked so long and hard to build was drying up. Harry could hardly stand it. In fact, the more that he thought of it, the sicker he got.

What would you do it you were in Harry's shoes?

_____

_____

_____

_____

My recommendations: Learn how to use the 90-second rapid self-hypnosis to calm yourself down. Also go through the exercises in this book that will help you to find a hidden identity, an identity that has calm, purpose, and adventure structured within it. At least three times a day, remind yourself of your hidden identity. Also, be sure to remind yourself to take total self-responsibility for the thoughts that you are choosing and the feelings and behavior that result.

A very effective thought for you right now is "Take the flames from the past and forget the ashes." Realize that the old days of the business might be gone forever. Grieve immediately for that. Go rapidly through denial, bargaining, anger, and depression and then get on with it. Join in times of today instead of dwelling on the past.

Here are some other effective thoughts for you:

"Be realistic, not merely reasonable" about your partner and other people in this world. This world is just not always a fair place.

"You can influence your partner, but you most certainly don't control him." You never should have sold him an equal share of the partnership in the first place. You should have kept 51 percent of it for yourself. But since that is history now, all you can do is influence.

"Take life enjoyment seriously and work as a game."

"You are not your reputation. Your reputation is an image, based on the way that someone else sees you. And you're not in charge of that. If someone really wanted to get to know you, they would find that you are the same old honest Harry that they used to know."

Once Harry began using his hidden identity (Mountain High), his eyes softened, his shoulders straightened, and he began to look years younger. And he began to take charge, not only of his inner life, but of Eagen and the business as well. "Eagen learned to treat me the way that I taught him to treat me. And I've taught him, slowly at first, but faster now, that he's got to treat both me and this business with deference and respect."

Case Number Five: Kenneth

After years of hard work, Kenneth Johnson had earned a reputation as one of the best tax experts in the country. But his talent and drive had made him a prisoner of his own success.

Every year, during the rush of the tax season he came under severe pressure—from his company, his clients, even from home, but mostly from himself. There never seemed enough time to do things as perfectly as Kenneth wanted. He often worked literally through the night, especially when there was a deadline. And in his business there were plenty of deadlines. Kenneth would never never let one of his client's down.

Ken believed that it was this dedication, commitment to the task at hand that led him to excel. And excel he did, far above his colleagues. He led the pack. The problem was, of course, the strain.

It was that last medical checkup that really frightened him. "Very high blood pressure. Danger of heart attack," the doctor said. But he couldn't seem to stop. Ken's demands on himself kept him ensnared in a kind of golden trap.

Then, during the first week in April, Ken found himself talking on one phone to the head of finance for XYZ while on the other phone the president of QRS was pressing him for "urgent information." Seated in his office was the firm's attorney, with essential questions. Later that evening, driving home, it happened: heart attack.

Ken's line of *defective* thinking (greatly condensed) went something like this:

I worry a lot about what others think of me. That's why I have to be the best tax accountant around. I can't change. That's me. I was always this way, and I'll always be this way. I find that I'm always under the gun—always acting. I work so hard, I think, because I've just got to succeed, to be the best. Failure is doom for me. I keep working very hard, because if I don't, the worst will happen.

I'm a natural born worrier. But at least I am a great tax accountant. That's who I am. A great tax accountant. And that's plenty. I got to keep moving, or the competition will be gaining on me. I've got to do well. I have no choice, what with my wife and my kids depending on me. I want to do everything well. I love to please everyone. That's my nature. I'm a reasonable man. Life should be reasonable as well. Don't you agree? But I'm under stress—It goes with the territory. I'm a responsible person and lot's of people depend on me. I like to play once in a while, then I work even harder to make up for it. Yep, that's me, Ken Johnson—the worry wart.

The medical prognosis was good. "No permanent damage, Kenneth, but you'll have to make major changes in your lifestyle," the doctor said.
What would you do if you were Kenneth?

_____

_____

_____

_____

My recommendations: It's quite possible that you can continue in the same business and do the very same kind of hectic work, but without experiencing the same kind of pressures. Make two lists each day, one for "urgent things" and the other for "urgent and important things." On his "urgent and important" list I would tell Kenneth to write: "become less stressed."

I identified a number of effective thoughts that might suit Ken, but the one that seemed to be most meaningful to him had to do with hidden identity. It seems that Ken got most of his identity from being known as an outstanding tax accountant. Once he learned how to develop and utilize a backup hidden identity that didn't depend on job title—much of the stress that he put on himself was relieved. And with the relief of stress came better health—and the chance to choose all of the other very effective thoughts that each of us are capable of pausing and choosing each day.

I said to Ken, "You have become a victim of your own good reputation. You see yourself as top tax accountant. And that identity is making you a nervous wreck. Get immediately in touch with your inner identity, one that has calm, purpose, and adventure. Stop, depending on your job title to know who you are."

What About the Quality of Your Own Work Life?

Most work-related problems fall into one of two categories: issues involving insufficient job competency and work skills, and issues related to unfairness and injustice.

What difficult issues are you currently facing? Review the two checklists here. Put one checkmark next to issues that give you some concern and a double checkmark next to those that give you more than a little concern. And, if something is seriously interfering with your goal of uncommon success, put three checkmarks.

WORKPLACE ISSUES CHECKLIST:
"COMPETENCIES AND SKILLS"

_____   Interpersonal communication
_____   Dealing with boss
_____   Dealing with a colleague
_____   Dealing with a subordinate
_____   Making presentations
_____   The presentation of self (image)
_____   Handling rejection
_____   Being sufficiently assertive
_____   Handling stress
_____   Managing time
_____   Avoiding procrastination
_____   Meeting deadlines
_____   Making sales (in house or external)
_____   Being a good team member
_____   Leadership
_____   Followership
_____   Enjoying the work itself
_____   Doing aspects of the work itself
_____   Dealing with perfectionism
_____   Dealing with impatience

WORKPLACE ISSUES CHECKLIST:
"FAIRNESS AND JUSTICE"

_____ Getting appropriate raises
_____ Getting a deserved promotion
_____ Dealing with difficult working conditions
_____ Having sufficient opportunity for advancement
_____ Earning enough money
_____ Having sufficient fringe benefits
_____ Dealing with firings, layoffs, cutbacks
_____ Being overworked
_____ Being taken for granted
_____ Coping with harassment, quotas, or prejudices concerning age, race, ethnicity, religion, or gender
_____ Other _____

_____

_____

_____

_____

Your job now is to apply the four steps of the ET process to the issues you've identified. Take each issue on, one at a time, on your own path to uncommon success.

Chapter 8

Uncommon Success: A Lifetime Habit

[First part of chapter shows how to use the ET process to help with difficult aspect of your personal life. Examines success dimension #3, a high level of personal life satisfaction. Describes actual cases. The second part of the chapter presents a composite description of the USP. Characteristics that are worthy objectives are listed, along with some self-defeating characteristics that you should avoid. Summarizes key elements of the ET process. Presents some useful ways to remind yourself to make uncommon success and the consistent use of the ET process a lifetime habit.]

The ET process applies just as much to your personal life as it does to your professional life. Personal life issues includes such matters as breakdowns in interpersonal relationships, lack of self-esteem, coping with divorce or separation, and raising children. In this chapter you will see how to use the ET process to give you a highly satisfying personal life, even under the most difficult circumstances.

USP Patrick Kelsey, a hard-working engineer, found that his wife, was extremely resentful of all the time he put in on his job. He describes how he handled this difficult personal life situation:

> I explained to Beverly that my work has become infinitely more demanding since I became a project

The ET Process for Uncommon Success

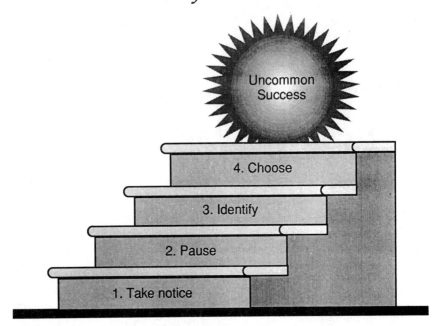

Put the Four Steps of the ET Process to Work in Your Personal Life

director. I sat down and carefully explained exactly what it was about the job that was taking so much of my time. I invited her to visit me at work so that she could actually see and get the feel for what it was that I am doing. I wanted her to appreciate my situation. And I extended myself a bit to see to it that I didn't shortchange her by slacking off on my share of the household chores that we both share.

In personal issues as well as work issues, success comes from attitude plus action. Patrick took effective action, and he also held onto an excellent attitude.

Since I have an absolute commitment to have a highly satisfying personal life, I must make certain that I do not become unduly upset just because Beverly is unhappy with me right now. I listen to her feelings. I'm doing all I can to help her to understand the realities of the situation. I will definitely not panic and start to feel guilty. If she convinces me that I don't have to put in as much time on the job as I am doing, I will listen to her. The one thing that I will not do is accept undue guilt, or act rash or uncaring, or panic. If I don't make this difficult period of my personal life highly satisfying for myself, I'd have nobody but myself to blame.

USPs decide well in advance of a crisis or pressure situation that they are determined to have a highly satisfying personal life, regardless of external circumstances. They are realistic; they know they have only a limited control over external circumstances. But they continuously remind themselves that they, and they alone, produce the quality of their personal satisfaction.

Difficulties seem to come in bunches. If a USP has one

problem come on top of another, he simply tells that problem to get in line, and then he solves it in turn. If the problem is an emergency, he gives it a priority number, and he uses the ET process to solve it when the time is appropriate.

Elaine has just discovered that her father has serious heart disease; his days are surely numbered. On top of that, she has been told that she has very high blood pressure and must go on a strict diet. As if that wasn't enough, her mother-in-law is coming up from Florida for another one of her long visits. Elaine's father died just few months after the diagnosis. Elaine grieved very deeply, but for only a limited time. Then, as quickly as possible, she came to accept the loss and moved into forward gear with her own life. She knows she has to attend to her own health, and that's her priority now. And when Elaine's mother-in-law came to visit, she simply tuned out her incessant chatter, and in fact found much to enjoy in the extended visit. Elaine has a policy of taking care of all of her issues, one by one—and only one at a time. When issues mount up, she gives them a number (as in the supermarket) and requires that each wait its turn.

USPs are certainly not saints, nor are they excluded from the hardships of life. But because of their uncommon way of thinking, they are better equipped than most to turn difficult situations around.

Case Histories

For each of the following cases once again, imagine that you are the person involved. After you have written down what you would do, I will, as before, share my own recommendations.

Case Number One: Alex

Alex Olin, forty-one, has been president of ABC Company for three years. Before that, he had always worked in the family-owned manufacturing business that his grandfather started. Alex loved the family business, but when it was sold to a Japanese company, Alex had to make a choice: stay with the family business under Japanese ownership or look elsewhere. Alex elected to move out. When ABC Company offered him the presidency, Alex called his wife and three children together. He wanted it to be a family decision. "Either we stay in town and I work for the new owners—or move to the mountains of Virginia where I'll be the president of ABC. I like the challenge, but it's up to all of you. Do we go? Or do we stay put?" The family voted: Leave.

Everything looked fine at first, but it wasn't long before Alex realized that the move was a major mistake. The ABC employees resented a newcomer coming in; it would be a long, tough job to win them over. His wife and children found this small, isolated mountain community very cool and hard to break in to. Alex's wife, Julie, felt so lost and isolated that she suffered a nervous breakdown, and the three children were having similar adjustment problems in school and their social life.

"This move has been a tougher nut to crack than I ever thought it would be," Alex said.

Alex was, of course, doing some very defective thinking that needed remediation. Here is a condensation of some his defective thinking:

I should never have had my family move in the first place. I feel so damned guilty. Guilty over what I've done to my wife. Guilty over the pressure that I've subjected my children to. I see no value is this pain that I feel. Yet I need to be a company president. It's always been expected of me. More than that, it's something that I've always expected for myself. I've got to make good. I have just got to. But I can get over how good we all had it before. Why did I ever leave and get us all into this rotten mess? I like to think of myself as a reasonably calm person who can handle almost anything. But all this is just a little too much. And it's beginning to get the best of me. Any ideas?

What you would do if you were Alex?

_____

_____

_____

_____

My recommended approach: Choose this extraordinarily useful effective thought: "Give me the courage to change the things I can change, the strength to accept those things over which I have little or no control, and the wisdom to know the difference."

You can definitely change your present line of defective thinking. Remember, your guilt-producing thoughts are making you feel guilty. And since guilt, especially after the fact, is useless, please stop. Remember, it was a family decision to make the move.

Your wife's nervous breakdown is a very serious matter, and you must do all that you can possibly do to help her. But don't forget that you will eventually have to take self-responsibility for your own nervous condition as well, if you allow yourself to fall apart.

The tendency to blame "the town" or "ABC Company" or "those uncaring people in this small mountain town" is normal and quite understandable—but not effective. It is your own thoughts about those things that are upsetting you and your family—and nothing else.

Finish grieving once and for all for the way things used to be. Then get busy identifying your options. Explore the possibility of meeting with school personnel and getting your children the extra help they desperately need. Plan some interventions to help your wife. Explore the possibility of resigning from ABC and taking a lower-level position in your hometown. Use your hidden identity so that you do not have to rely on the job title "president" to define who you really are.

Most of Alex's issues were resolved over the course of time. His wife Julie and children did eventually adjust to the new town. It took some effective thinking on their part too, of course. Julie learned to choose effective thoughts to deal with depression, the future, hurting, identity, and realistic expectations. Alex helped her, not by insisting or lecturing, but by setting an example of someone who can take a high level of self-responsibility. As Julie became more comfortable with herself, she became more comfortable to be with for others as well. And together, she and Alex set a very powerful example for their children, who also learned how to do effective thinking.

Alex eventually won over his employees—his enthusiasm and caring ways were contagious. He chose effective thoughts about listening, influencing others, caring, and other effective thoughts pertaining to management. He had the persistency and the stamina, armed with the tactics learned through effective thinking—to become an uncommonly successful CEO, husband, and father.

Case Number Two: Annette

Annette Baxter was thirty-three and single. She was the buyer for a national chain of high-fashion retail stores. Her job required lots of travel, leaving little time for social life. Her string of defective thoughts went something like this:

All this traveling, all these hours working, has just about killed off my social life. In fact, I have no social life to speak of. Here I am: Thirty-three years old, a successful career, prestige, best hotels, world travel, power—all the trappings of success and, yet, deep down, I'm miserable. No social life. No man in my life. I think that I've really made a mess of my life. I'm afraid of being hurt. I can't stand being rejected. I desperately need to be very, very close to a special person, but I'm afraid to take chances, to expose myself. I'm a bit of a cynic about men anyway. Failure in another relationship will destroy me. Isn't there any justice? I think I deserve a better fate. My outlook isn't very optimistic, when it comes to men. You see, in order to date and all that you have to play games, and I'm not into games. Anyway, my job takes all my time. And that keeps me from risking and being hurt. I feel that my purpose in life is to do a great job for my company, to excel at what I do. And I do. But something is missing. I really need a great, intimate, growing relationship with someone from the opposite sex. That's what I need.

What you would do if you were Annette?

_____

_____

_____

_____

_____

_____

_____

My recommendations to Annette: You are certainly at a point in your life where you have to make some decisions. Do you want to continue the kind of career that you've been pursuing, or go for a more balanced existence? If you want to develop a closer relationship with a special man, then you have got to risk being hurt. Using the ET Process, you'll be able to get over any setback in rapid fashion, so stick your neck out and start dating. Call and ask a man out on a date, if you see one who is appealing to you. Choose this thought: "I prefer a warm and loving relationship. I don't really need it to survive, but I most certainly prefer it."

On one of her buying trips in Europe Annette opened a conversation with a man seated next to her on the flight. One thing led to the next, and now they are actively dating. "He may not be the man I'm going to marry, but we are having a wonderful time together."

Case Number Three: Sid

Sid Edwards, through no fault of his own, was out of a job. His savings were providing just the barest necessities for his wife and children. His wife and children actually went to bed hungry most nights. "My situation is just about as miserable as it possibly could be," he said. "All I need now is to get cancer and the picture will be complete. I just don't know what to do. How about some help? The hell with your ET Process, I just want to *survive!*"

What you would do, if you were Sid?

_____

_____

_____

_____

_____

_____

My advice: No question about it, Sid, you have more than your share of misery. But the ET process is also a process for surviving. I know that you are talking poverty—real, not imaginary, misery. But let me tell you that you and you alone are responsible for how miserable you feel—with or without a job. Of course you have the right to feel completely miserable, but do you want to? What if you were to face your losses and get finished grieving for your awful predicament, and then decide to get on with your life?

It took six months of job-seeking action before Sid and his family got back on their feet. But during those six months, Sid, because he learned the ET process, refused to suffer. "It makes no sense to waste time suffering when I've got so many other more worthwhile and important things to do."

Case Number Four: Alan

It seemed that Alan was perpetually trying to shed "those ten extra pounds." The only problem was, every time he succeeded, he seemed to gain fifteen back. No matter what his weight was, he never was satisfied. Alan's string of defective thoughts were as follows:

> If I get satisfied, and accept myself as I am, that would be settling for imperfection. I'm not a perfectionist in everything that I do, but I guess I am when it comes to my body. Let's face it. My looks are important to me. And I never seem to be satisfied. When I look in the mirror, I just don't like what I see. It seems I'm always on a diet, trying to lose just 10 more pounds. I want to be perfect. This dieting, dieting, dieting is driving me crazy. It seems as if there's nothing I can do about it. I think it's my body type and fat cells. I think my mother fed me too much when I was little and now I'm stuck with too many fat cells. Damn you, mother. I think I'm a total failure when it comes to getting down to the weight I deserve. I just keep sabotaging my diet,

because I want to punish myself. Fat guy: That's who I am. But that's not who I want to be. I get so jealous when I see my friends lose weight and keep it off. It kills me. I need to lose this ten pounds. I really need to do it. I look awful. When I do that, I'll be so happy. Too bad fattening foods always look so good and make me lose control. What a battle.

How you would use the ET Process to help yourself if you were Alan?

_____

_____

_____

_____

_____

My advice: Recognize that your perfectionist standards about your weight are very defective thoughts. Replace them with this effective thought: "I just want to look excellent, not perfect." Use the 90-second rapid self-hypnosis method to get that one thought into your subconscious.

Once he gave up his unrealistic goal of perfection, Alan was able to shed fifteen pounds, and he has kept them off for more than six years.

Check the Quality of Your Personal Life

The Effective Thinking process can help you with any personal issue that gives you difficulty. Look over this checklist. If you find items that remind you of issues you are facing, take notice. Then attack each one of them systematically, one by one, using the ET process. Get yourself back on the path to uncommon success by mobilizing all you've learned in this book and put it immediately to work for you.

Some Possible Sources for Interpersonal Issues

_____ Friend
_____ Family member
_____ Neighbor
_____ Parents
_____ Children
_____ Spouse

Some Possible Self-Esteem Issues

_____ Your past
_____ Your present
_____ Your appearance
_____ Your weight
_____ Your intellect
_____ Your personality
_____ Smoking
_____ Drinking
_____ Drug abuse

Some Possible Marriage-Related Issues

_____ Finances
_____ Child rearing
_____ Communication
_____ In-laws
_____ Divorce or separation
_____ Fidelity
_____ Sexual problems

Some Possible Physical Health Issues

_____ Illness and disease
_____ Diet and exercise

_____   Medication
_____   Surgery

Some Possible Mental Health Issues

_____   Compulsiveness
_____   Worry
_____   Fear
_____   Jealousy
_____   Excessive anger
_____   Confusion
_____   Procrastination
_____   Forgetfulness
_____   Neuroses
_____   Psychoses

Some of the Larger Social Issues

_____   Political upsets and upheaval
_____   Prejudices
_____   Poverty and homelessness
_____   Wars
_____   Riots
_____   Hunger
_____   Corruption

You Now Qualify for Full Membership in the USP Club

By applying the four-step effective thinking process to your issues, you have in hand all you will ever need to remain a fully qualified member of the 4 percent club—a certified USP. Let's take a look at your fellow members.

A Composite Description of USPs

USP come from all walks of life and are found equally among all races, religions, and sexual and philosophical persuasions.

They are found equally among males and females, and are located throughout the world. They can be found in the full range of work settings in all kinds of occupations. Some USPs are white-collar workers, others blue-collar. They are practically everywhere—as long as the work they do is honest and legitimate.

All USPs excel at their work *and* they genuinely enjoy it, even when circumstances get tough. They take their job seriously, but job satisfaction even more seriously. In addition, USPs have very rich and satisfying personal lives, even in the face of some extreme difficulties. They're not saints, but they see to it that they have an excellent attitude for both very good and very difficult situations. That's because they take total self-responsibility and see themselves as thought choosers rather than mere receptacles for the thoughts of others.

One USP club member, Ron Murphy, an insurance company executive, calls himself "an attitude thief."

Look, I've always been a very competitive person and it is this strong sense of competitiveness has most certainly helped me to move to the top in my particular field. But competition, as you know, can be very destructive unless you compete for something that really makes sense. A few years ago, I found a very useful outlet for my competitive ways that has really been the key to my continuing success. I learned to chase and collect marvelous attitudes. If I find someone with a better attitude than I have for any given situation, I really listen to that person. And then, if I really want it, I just steal it and take it for my own and add it to my collection. And then when the time comes that I need just that attitude, I've got it ready to go. I use marvelous attitudes all the time. It's one of the world's great free resources.

USPs do not merely adjust to difficult situations. They do not graciously turn the other cheek in the face of difficulty, but instead do everything humanly possible to change things. But in those rare instances where a change is not possible, then, they choose thoughts that allow themselves to make the best of the circumstance.

To help them handle any difficulty in their personal or professional life, USPs make use of a hidden identity. This hidden identity goes far beyond their given name, their job title, and even their family role. They use this hidden identity to keep themselves on an even keel whenever their work life or their personal life becomes especially difficult. Their hidden identity provides them with a clear self-picture that includes three very important qualtities: inner calm, clarity of purpose, and adventure. This "backup" identity enables them to remain calm when others about them have become tense and upset.

USP Do's and Don'ts

To become the best possible USP, there are certain characteristics you want to continue to develop, and other traits you will strive to eliminate.

Do be

- Realistic and down-to-earth
- Worthy of the trust of others
- A high performer, especially on the particular aspects of the job that you have decided to focus on
- Self-responsible, especially when it comes to your own thoughts, feelings, and behavior
- A high achiever
- Able to live a psychologically rich and satisfying life
- Caring and loving of others

- Actively engaged in a project that is important (at least in your own eyes)
- Self-respectful
- Respectful of authority (but never blindly obedient)
- In possession of a good sense of humor, especially in the face of life's inevitable difficulties
- Compulsive and addictive when it comes to applying the ET process
- Capable of "creative worry" or due concern, as needed
- Capable of becoming "creatively depressed" whenever it makes sense to become that way
- Capable of "creative anger," when anger serves a useful purpose, as it sometimes does
- Capable of "creative self-deception," as needed
- Able to enjoy a combination of inner calm, clarity of personal purpose, and adventure (by using your hidden identity)
- A healthy skeptic but never a cynic
- "Happy" but mostly as a byproduct of satisfaction
- In touch with your fundamental sense of "existential loneliness," to help you to clarify your own unique purpose in life
- Sensual, making maximum use of all of your natural senses
- A wise risk taker
- A role player, whenever it makes sense to play a role really well
- A sensitive and caring listener

Don't be

- A saint
- A "Pollyanna" positive thinker
- Desperate for happiness—seek life satisfaction instead
- Disloyal or untrustworthy

- Nonspiritual
- Wooden, uncaring, or cold
- Always in control (that would make you a robot)

In short, use the ET Process to make your personal and professional life as rich and as satisfying as possible—and never at the expense of any other person. Change what needs to be changed, if at all possible, and accept what can't be changed as good-naturedly as you can.

Eleven Useful Questions

Now and again remind yourself of the fundamentals of the ET process with these eleven questions.

1. What is your main goal in life? *Answer:* To have uncommon success and all that that implies.
2. Who chooses your thoughts? *Answer:* I do.
3. Who are you? *Answer:* [My hidden identity]
4. What are you? *Answer* (always the same): A thought chooser.
5. Why are you? *Answer:* To have a rich and satisfying, uncommonly successful life.
6. Where are you? *Answer* (always the same): Here. *Followup question:* How do you make your here's uncommonly successful? *Answer:* By using the ET process.
7. When are you? *Answer:* Now. *Followup question:* How do you make your nows uncommonly successful? *Answer:* By using the ET process.
8. What are the four steps of the ET process. *Answer:* Take notice, pause, identify, and choose. *Followup question:* Can you state the ET process in one brief sentence. *Answer:* Whenever necessary, pause then identify and choose effective thoughts.
9. What are the five steps of getting over any loss or

setback as rapidly and as healthily as possible? *Answer:* Denial, bargaining, anger, depression, and—just as soon as possible—acceptance.
10. What are the four steps in 90-second rapid self-hypnosis? *Answer:* Relax, creative self-deception, enter the effective thought, three times, then wake up reprogrammed.
11. What are three recommended methods for choosing effective thoughts? *Answer:* Direct free will, reverse psychology, and self-hypnosis to reach the subconscious.

Becoming and Remaining Uncommonly Successful

Use the ET process frequently, and eventually it will become a habit. Remember, you have full responsibility for the thoughts that you choose and the feelings and behavior that result from those thoughts. If the thoughts that you consistently choose as a matter of habit are effective thoughts, rather than defective ones, you are bound to achieve a life that is rich and satisfying. The life of a USP club member. Welcome aboard.

Index

[Page numbers in italics refer to figures.]